OTHELLO,
THE MOOR OF VENICE.

OTHELLO,
THE MOOR OF VENICE

BY

WILLIAM SHAKESPEARE

1870 EDITION

ORIGINALLY WRITTEN IN 1603

ILLUSTRATED by H. C. SELOUS

ILLUSTRATED PLAYS OF
WILLIAM SHAKESPEARE
PUBLISHED BY

SEAWOLF
PRESS

OTHELLO, THE MOOR OF VENICE

PUBLISHED BY SEAWOLF PRESS

EDITION INFORMATION

The illustrations are by H. C. Selous. The cover is based on a 19th century painting entitled "Othello and Desdemona" by Daniel Maclise.

PERMISSIONS

The 19 illustrations appearing in this publication, including the frontispiece, are courtesy of Michael John Goodman, The Victorian Illustrated Shakespeare Archive, January 20, 2019. They are drawn by H.C. Selous and appeared in the 1870 Cassell & Company printing of *The Plays of William Shakespeare*.

SeaWolf Press
P.O. Box 961
Orinda, CA 94563
Email: support@seawolfpress.com
Web: http://www.SeaWolfPress.com

CONTENTS

ACT I.

ACT II.

ACT III.

ACT IV.

ACT V.

Dramatis Personæ

DUKE OF VENICE.
BRABANTIO, a Senator.
Other Senators.
GRATIANO, Brother to Brabantio.
LODOVICO, Kinsman to Brabantio.
OTHELLO, a noble Moor, in the service of Venice.
CASSIO, his Lieutenant.
IAGO, his Ancient.
RODERIGO, a Venetian Gentleman.
MONTANO, Othello's predecessor in the government of Cyprus.
CLOWN, Servant to Othello.
Herald.
DESDEMONA, Daughter to Brabantio and Wife to Othello.
EMILIA, Wife to Iago.
BIANCA, Mistress to Cassio.

Officers, Gentlemen, Messenger, Musicians, Herald, Sailor,
Attendants, &c.

SCENE: *The First Act in Venice; during the rest of the Play at a
Seaport in Cyprus.*

ACT I.

SCENE I. *Venice. A street.*

Enter Roderigo *and* Iago.

RODERIGO.

Tush, never tell me; I take it much unkindly
That thou, Iago, who hast had my purse
As if the strings were thine, shouldst know of this,—

IAGO.

'Sblood, but you will not hear me:—
If ever I did dream of such a matter,
Abhor me.

RODERIGO.

Thou told'st me thou didst hold him in thy hate.

IAGO.

Despise me, if I do not. Three great ones of the city,
In personal suit to make me his lieutenant,
Off-capp'd to him:—and, by the faith of man,
I know my price, I am worth no worse a place:—
But he, as loving his own pride and purposes,
Evades them, with a bumbast circumstance
Horribly stuff'd with epithets of war:
And, in conclusion, nonsuits
My mediators: for, "Certes," says he,
"I have already chose my officer."
And what was he?
Forsooth, a great arithmetician,
One Michael Cassio, a Florentine,
A fellow almost damn'd in a fair wife;

That never set a squadron in the field,
Nor the division of a battle knows
More than a spinster; unless the bookish theoric,
Wherein the toged consuls can propose
As masterly as he: mere prattle, without practice,
Is all his soldiership. But he, sir, had the election:
And I,—of whom his eyes had seen the proof
At Rhodes, at Cyprus, and on other grounds,
Christian and heathen,—must be belee'd and calm'd
By debitor and creditor, this counter-caster;
He, in good time, must his lieutenant be,
And I—God bless the mark! his Moorship's ancient.

Roderigo.

By heaven, I rather would have been his hangman.

Iago.

Why, there's no remedy; 'tis the curse of service,
Preferment goes by letter and affection,
And not by old gradation, where each second
Stood heir to the first. Now, sir, be judge yourself
Whether I in any just term am affin'd
To love the Moor.

Roderigo.

I would not follow him, then.

Iago.

O, sir, content you;
I follow him to serve my turn upon him:
We cannot all be masters, nor all masters
Cannot be truly follow'd. You shall mark
Many a duteous and knee-crooking knave
That, doting on his own obsequious bondage,
Wears out his time, much like his master's ass,
For nought but provender; and when he's old, cashier'd:
Whip me such honest knaves. Others there are
Who, trimm'd in forms and visages of duty,
Keep yet their hearts attending on themselves;
And, throwing but shows of service on their lords,
Do well thrive by them, and when they have lin'd their coats,
Do themselves homage: these fellows have some soul;
And such a one do I profess myself. For, sir,
It is as sure as you are Roderigo,
Were I the Moor, I would not be Iago:

In following him, I follow but myself;
Heaven is my judge, not I for love and duty,
But seeming so for my peculiar end:
For when my outward action doth demonstrate
The native act and figure of my heart
In complement extern, 'tis not long after
But I will wear my heart upon my sleeve
For daws to peck at: I am not what I am.

Roderigo. What, ho, Brabantio! Signior Brabantio, ho!

Act I. Scene I.

RODERIGO.

What a full fortune does the thick lips owe,
If he can carry't thus!

IAGO.

Call up her father,
Rouse him:—make after him, poison his delight,
Proclaim him in the streets; incense her kinsmen,
And, though he in a fertile climate dwell,
Plague him with flies: though that his joy be joy,
Yet throw such changes of vexation on't
As it may lose some color.

RODERIGO.

Here is her father's house: I'll call aloud.

IAGO.

Do; with like timorous accent and dire yell
As when, by night and negligence, the fire
Is spied in populous cities.

RODERIGO.

What, ho, Brabantio! Signior Brabantio, ho!

IAGO.

Awake! what, ho, Brabantio! thieves! thieves! thieves!
Look to your house, your daughter, and your bags!
Thieves! thieves!

[BRABANTIO appears above at a window.]

BRABANTIO.

What is the reason of this terrible summons?
What is the matter there?

RODERIGO.

Signior, is all your family within?

IAGO.

Are your doors locked?

BRABANTIO.

Why, wherefore ask you this?

IAGO.

Zounds, sir, you're robb'd; for shame, put on your gown;
Your heart is burst, you have lost half your soul;
Even now, now, very now, an old black ram
Is tupping your white ewe. Arise, arise;
Awake the snorting citizens with the bell,
Or else the devil will make a grandsire of you:
Arise, I say.

BRABANTIO.

What, have you lost your wits?

RODERIGO.

Most reverend signior, do you know my voice?

BRABANTIO.

Not I; what are you?

RODERIGO.

My name is Roderigo.

BRABANTIO.

The worser welcome:
I have charged thee not to haunt about my doors;
In honest plainness thou hast heard me say
My daughter is not for thee; and now, in madness,
Being full of supper and distempering draughts,
Upon malicious bravery dost thou come
To start my quiet.

RODERIGO.

Sir, sir, sir,—

BRABANTIO.

But thou must needs be sure
My spirit and my place have in them power
To make this bitter to thee.

RODERIGO.

Patience, good sir.

BRABANTIO.

What tell'st thou me of robbing? this is Venice;
My house is not a grange.

RODERIGO.

Most grave Brabantio,
In simple and pure soul I come to you.

IAGO.

Zounds, sir, you are one of those that will not serve God if the devil
bid you. Because we come to do you service, and you think we are
ruffians, you'll have your daughter covered with a Barbary horse;
you'll have your nephews neigh to you; you'll have coursers for
cousins and gennets for germans.

BRABANTIO.

What profane wretch art thou?

IAGO.

I am one, sir, that comes to tell you your daughter and the Moor
are now making the beast with two backs.

BRABANTIO.

Thou art a villain.

IAGO.

You are—a senator.

BRABANTIO.

This thou shalt answer; I know thee, Roderigo.

RODERIGO.

Sir, I will answer anything. But, I beseech you,
If't be your pleasure and most wise consent,—
As partly I find it is,—that your fair daughter,
At this odd-even and dull watch o' the night,
Transported with no worse nor better guard
But with a knave of common hire, a gondolier,
To the gross clasps of a lascivious Moor,—
If this be known to you, and your allowance,
We then have done you bold and saucy wrongs;
But if you know not this, my manners tell me
We have your wrong rebuke. Do not believe
That, from the sense of all civility,
I thus would play and trifle with your reverence:
Your daughter,—if you have not given her leave,—
I say again, hath made a gross revolt;
Tying her duty, beauty, wit, and fortunes
In an extravagant and wheeling stranger
Of here and everywhere. Straight satisfy yourself:
If she be in her chamber or your house
Let loose on me the justice of the state
For thus deluding you.

BRABANTIO.

Strike on the tinder, ho!
Give me a taper!—Call up all my people!—
This accident is not unlike my dream:
Belief of it oppresses me already.—
Light, I say! light!

[Exit from above.

IAGO.

Farewell; for I must leave you:
It seems not meet nor wholesome to my place
To be produc'd,—as if I stay I shall,—
Against the Moor: for I do know the state,—
However this may gall him with some check,—

Cannot with safety cast him; for he's embark'd
With such loud reason to the Cyprus wars,—
Which even now stand in act,—that, for their souls,
Another of his fathom they have none
To lead their business: in which regard,
Though I do hate him as I do hell pains,
Yet, for necessity of present life,
I must show out a flag and sign of love,
Which is indeed but sign. That you shall surely find him,
Lead to the Sagittary the raised search;
And there will I be with him. So, farewell.

[Exit.

Enter, below, BRABANTIO, *and Servants with torches.*

BRABANTIO.

It is too true an evil: gone she is;
And what's to come of my despised time
Is naught but bitterness.—Now, Roderigo,
Where didst thou see her?—O unhappy girl!—
With the Moor, say'st thou?—Who would be a father!
How didst thou know 'twas she?—O, she deceives me
Past thought.—What said she to you?—Get more tapers;
Raise all my kindred.—Are they married, think you?

RODERIGO.

Truly, I think they are.

BRABANTIO.

O heaven!—How got she out?—O treason of the blood!—
Fathers, from hence trust not your daughters' minds
By what you see them act.—Are there not charms
By which the property of youth and maidhood
May be abused? Have you not read, Roderigo,
Of some such thing?

RODERIGO.

Yes, sir, I have indeed.

BRABANTIO.

Call up my brother.—O, would you had had her!—
Some one way, some another.—Do you know
Where we may apprehend her and the Moor?

RODERIGO.

I think I can discover him, if you please
To get good guard, and go along with me.

BRABANTIO.

Pray you, lead on. At every house I'll call;
I may command at most.—Get weapons, ho!
And raise some special officers of night.—
On, good Roderigo:—I'll deserve your pains.

[*Exeunt.*

SCENE II. *Venice. Another street.*

Enter OTHELLO, IAGO, *and Attendants with torches.*

IAGO.

Though in the trade of war I have slain men,
Yet do I hold it very stuff o' the conscience
To do no contriv'd murder: I lack iniquity
Sometimes to do me service: nine or ten times
I had thought to have yerk'd him here under the ribs.

OTHELLO.

'Tis better as it is.

IAGO.

Nay, but he prated,
And spoke such scurvy and provoking terms
Against your honor,
That, with the little godliness I have,
I did full hard forbear him. But, I pray you, sir,
Are you fast married? Be assured of this,
That the magnifico is much beloved;
And hath, in his effect, a voice potential
As double as the duke's: he will divorce you;
Or put upon you what restraint and grievance
The law,—with all his might to enforce it on,—
Will give him cable.

OTHELLO.

Let him do his spite:
My services which I have done the signiory
Shall out-tongue his complaints. 'Tis yet to know,—
Which, when I know that boasting is an honor,

I shall promulgate,—I fetch my life and being
From men of royal siege; and my demerits
May speak unbonneted to as proud a fortune
As this that I have reach'd: for know, Iago,
But that I love the gentle Desdemona,
I would not my unhoused free condition
Put into circumscription and confine
For the sea's worth. But, look! what lights come yond?

IAGO.

Those are the raised father and his friends:
You were best go in.

OTHELLO.

Not I; I must be found;
My parts, my title, and my perfect soul
Shall manifest me rightly. Is it they?

IAGO.

By Janus, I think no.

Enter CASSIO *and certain Officers with torches.*

OTHELLO.

The servants of the duke and my lieutenant.—
The goodness of the night upon you, friends!
What is the news?

CASSIO.

The duke does greet you, general;
And he requires your haste-post-haste appearance
Even on the instant.

OTHELLO.

What is the matter, think you?

CASSIO.

Something from Cyprus, as I may divine:
It is a business of some heat: the galleys
Have sent a dozen sequent messengers
This very night at one another's heels;
And many of the consuls, rais'd and met,
Are at the duke's already: you have been hotly call'd for;
When, being not at your lodging to be found,
The senate hath sent about three several quests
To search you out.

OTHELLO.

'Tis well I am found by you.
I will but spend a word here in the house,
And go with you.

[*Exit.*

CASSIO.

Ancient, what makes he here?

IAGO.

Faith, he to-night hath boarded a land carack:
If it prove lawful prize, he's made forever.

CASSIO.

I do not understand.

IAGO.

He's married.

CASSIO.

To who?

Re-enter OTHELLO.

IAGO.

Marry, to—Come, captain, will you go?

OTHELLO.

Have with you.

CASSIO.

Here comes another troop to seek for you.

IAGO.

It is Brabantio.—General, be advis'd;
He comes to bad intent.

Enter Brabantio, Roderigo, and Officers with torches and weapons.

OTHELLO.

Holla! stand there!

RODERIGO.

Signior, it is the Moor.

BRABANTIO.

Down with him, thief!
[*They draw on both sides.*]

IAGO.

You, Roderigo! come, sir, I am for you.

Iago. You, Roderigo! come, sir, I am for you.
Othello. Keep up your bright swords, for the dew will rust them.
                                    Act I. Scene II.

OTHELLO.

Keep up your bright swords, for the dew will rust them.—
Good signior, you shall more command with years
Than with your weapons.

BRABANTIO.

O thou foul thief, where hast thou stow'd my daughter?
Damn'd as thou art, thou hast enchanted her;
For I'll refer me to all things of sense,
If she in chains of magic were not bound,
Whether a maid so tender, fair, and happy,
So opposite to marriage that she shunn'd
The wealthy curled darlings of our nation,
Would ever have, to incur a general mock,
Run from her guardage to the sooty bosom
Of such a thing as thou,—to fear, not to delight.
Judge me the world, if 'tis not gross in sense
That thou hast practis'd on her with foul charms;
Abus'd her delicate youth with drugs or minerals
That weaken motion:—I'll have't disputed on;
'Tis probable, and palpable to thinking.
I therefore apprehend and do attach thee
For an abuser of the world, a practiser
Of arts inhibited and out of warrant.—
Lay hold upon him: if he do resist,
Subdue him at his peril.

OTHELLO.

Hold your hands,
Both you of my inclining and the rest:
Were it my cue to fight, I should have known it
Without a prompter.—Where will you that I go
To answer this your charge?

BRABANTIO.

To prison; till fit time
Of law and course of direct session
Call thee to answer.

OTHELLO.

What if I do obey?
How may the duke be therewith satisfied,
Whose messengers are here about my side,
Upon some present business of the state,
To bring me to him?

FIRST OFFICER.

'Tis true, most worthy signior;
The duke's in council, and your noble self,
I am sure, is sent for.

BRABANTIO.

How! the duke in council!
In this time of the night!—Bring him away:
Mine's not an idle cause: the duke himself,
Or any of my brothers of the state,
Cannot but feel this wrong as 'twere their own;
For if such actions may have passage free,
Bond slaves and pagans shall our statesmen be.

[Exeunt.

SCENE III. *Venice. A council chamber.*

[The DUKE *and Senators sitting at a table; Officers attending.]*

DUKE.

There is no composition in these news
That gives them credit.

FIRST SENATOR.

Indeed, they are disproportion'd;
My letters say a hundred and seven galleys.

DUKE.

And mine a hundred and forty.

SECOND SENATOR.

And mine two hundred:
But though they jump not on a just account,—
As in these cases, where the aim reports,
'Tis oft with difference,—yet do they all confirm
A Turkish fleet, and bearing up to Cyprus.

DUKE.

Nay, it is possible enough to judgement:
I do not so secure me in the error,
But the main article I do approve
In fearful sense.

SAILOR.

[Within.] What, ho! what, ho! what, ho!

FIRST OFFICER.

A messenger from the galleys.

Enter a SAILOR.

DUKE.

Now,—what's the business?

SAILOR.

The Turkish preparation makes for Rhodes;
So was I bid report here to the state
By Signior Angelo.

DUKE.

How say you by this change?

FIRST SENATOR.

This cannot be,
By no assay of reason: 'tis a pageant
To keep us in false gaze. When we consider
The importancy of Cyprus to the Turk;
And let ourselves again but understand
That, as it more concerns the Turk than Rhodes,
So may he with more facile question bear it,
For that it stands not in such warlike brace,
But altogether lacks the abilities
That Rhodes is dress'd in. If we make thought of this,
We must not think the Turk is so unskilful
To leave that latest which concerns him first;
Neglecting an attempt of ease and gain,
To wake and wage a danger profitless.

DUKE.

Nay, in all confidence, he's not for Rhodes.

FIRST OFFICER.

Here is more news.

Enter a MESSENGER.

MESSENGER.

The Ottomites, reverend and gracious,
Steering with due course toward the isle of Rhodes,
Have there injointed them with an after fleet.

FIRST SENATOR.

Ay, so I thought.—How many, as you guess?

MESSENGER.

Of thirty sail: and now they do re-stem
Their backward course, bearing with frank appearance
Their purposes toward Cyprus.—Signior Montano,

Your trusty and most valiant servitor,
With his free duty recommends you thus,
And prays you to believe him.

DUKE.

'Tis certain, then, for Cyprus.—
Marcus Luccicos, is not he in town?

FIRST SENATOR.

He's now in Florence.

DUKE.

Write from us to him; post-post-haste despatch.

FIRST SENATOR.

Here comes Brabantio and the valiant Moor.

Enter BRABANTIO, OTHELLO, IAGO, RODERIGO, *and Officers.*

DUKE.

Valiant Othello, we must straight employ you
Against the general enemy Ottoman.—
[To BRABANTIO.*]* I did not see you; welcome, gentle signior;
We lack'd your counsel and your help to-night.

BRABANTIO.

So did I yours. Good your grace, pardon me;
Neither my place, nor aught I heard of business
Hath rais'd me from my bed; nor doth the general care
Take hold on me; for my particular grief
Is of so flood-gate and o'erbearing nature
That it engluts and swallows other sorrows,
And it is still itself.

DUKE.

Why, what's the matter?

BRABANTIO.

My daughter! O, my daughter!

DUKE AND SENATORS.

Dead?

BRABANTIO.

Ay, to me;
She is abused, stol'n from me, and corrupted
By spells and medicines bought of mountebanks;
For nature so preposterously to err,

Being not deficient, blind, or lame of sense,
Sans witchcraft could not.

DUKE.

Whoe'er he be that, in this foul proceeding,
Hath thus beguiled your daughter of herself,
And you of her, the bloody book of law
You shall yourself read in the bitter letter
After your own sense; yea, though our proper son
Stood in your action.

BRABANTIO.

Humbly I thank your grace.
Here is the man, this Moor; whom now, it seems,
Your special mandate for the state affairs
Hath hither brought.

DUKE AND SENATORS.

We are very sorry for't.

DUKE.

[To OTHELLO.] What, in your own part, can you say to this?

BRABANTIO.

Nothing, but this is so.

OTHELLO.

Most potent, grave, and reverend signiors,
My very noble and approv'd good masters,—
That I have ta'en away this old man's daughter,
It is most true; true, I have married her:
The very head and front of my offending
Hath this extent, no more. Rude am I in my speech,
And little bless'd with the soft phrase of peace;
For since these arms of mine had seven years' pith,
Till now some nine moons wasted, they have us'd
Their dearest action in the tented field;
And little of this great world can I speak,
More than pertains to feats of broil and battle;
And therefore little shall I grace my cause
In speaking for myself. Yet, by your gracious patience,
I will a round unvarnish'd tale deliver
Of my whole course of love: what drugs, what charms,
What conjuration, and what mighty magic,—
For such proceeding I am charged withal,—
I won his daughter.

BRABANTIO.

A maiden never bold:
Of spirit so still and quiet that her motion
Blush'd at herself; and she,—in spite of nature,
Of years, of country, credit, everything,—
To fall in love with what she fear'd to look on!
It is judgement maim'd and most imperfect
That will confess perfection so could err
Against all rules of nature; and must be driven
To find out practices of cunning hell,
Why this should be. I therefore vouch again,
That with some mixtures powerful o'er the blood,
Or with some dram conjur'd to this effect,
He wrought upon her.

DUKE.

To vouch this is no proof;
Without more wider and more overt test
Than these thin habits and poor likelihoods
Of modern seeming do prefer against him.

FIRST SENATOR.

But, Othello, speak:
Did you by indirect and forced courses
Subdue and poison this young maid's affections?
Or came it by request, and such fair question
As soul to soul affordeth?

OTHELLO.

I do beseech you,
Send for the lady to the Sagittary,
And let her speak of me before her father.
If you do find me foul in her report,
The trust, the office I do hold of you,
Not only take away, but let your sentence
Even fall upon my life.

DUKE.

Fetch Desdemona hither.

OTHELLO.

Ancient, conduct them; you best know the place.—

[Exeunt IAGO *and Attendants.*

And, till she come, as truly as to heaven

I do confess the vices of my blood,
So justly to your grave ears I'll present
How I did thrive in this fair lady's love,
And she in mine.

DUKE.

Say it, Othello.

OTHELLO.

Her father lov'd me; oft invited me;
Still question'd me the story of my life,
From year to year,—the battles, sieges, fortunes,
That I have pass'd.
I ran it through, even from my boyish days
To the very moment that he bade me tell it:
Wherein I spake of most disastrous chances,
Of moving accidents by flood and field;
Of hair-breadth scapes i' the imminent deadly breach;
Of being taken by the insolent foe,
And sold to slavery; of my redemption thence,
And portance in my travels' history:
Wherein of antres vast and deserts idle,
Rough quarries, rocks, and hills whose heads touch heaven,
It was my hint to speak,—such was the process;
And of the Cannibals that each other eat,
The Anthropophagi, and men whose heads
Do grow beneath their shoulders. This to hear
Would Desdemona seriously incline:
But still the house affairs would draw her thence;
Which ever as she could with haste despatch,
She'd come again, and with a greedy ear
Devour up my discourse; which I observing,
Took once a pliant hour; and found good means
To draw from her a prayer of earnest heart
That I would all my pilgrimage dilate,
Whereof by parcels she had something heard,
But not intentively; I did consent;
And often did beguile her of her tears,
When I did speak of some distressful stroke
That my youth suffer'd. My story being done,
She gave me for my pains a world of sighs:
She swore,—in faith, 'twas strange, 'twas passing strange;
'Twas pitiful, 'twas wondrous pitiful:

She wish'd she had not heard it, yet she wish'd
That heaven had made her such a man: she thank'd me;
And bade me, if I had a friend that lov'd her,
I should but teach him how to tell my story,
And that would woo her. Upon this hint I spake:
She lov'd me for the dangers I had pass'd;
And I lov'd her that she did pity them.
This only is the witchcraft I have us'd:—
Here comes the lady; let her witness it.

Enter DESDEMONA, IAGO, *and Attendants.*

DUKE.

I think this tale would win my daughter too.—
Good Brabantio,
Take up this mangled matter at the best.
Men do their broken weapons rather use
Than their bare hands.

BRABANTIO.

I pray you, hear her speak:
If she confess that she was half the wooer,
Destruction on my head, if my bad blame
Light on the man!—Come hither, gentle mistress:
Do you perceive in all this noble company
Where most you owe obedience?

DESDEMONA.

My noble father,
I do perceive here a divided duty:
To you I am bound for life and education;
My life and education both do learn me
How to respect you; you are the lord of duty,—
I am hitherto your daughter: but here's my husband;
And so much duty as my mother show'd
To you, preferring you before her father,
So much I challenge that I may profess
Due to the Moor, my lord.

BRABANTIO.

God be with you!—I have done.—
Please it your grace, on to the state affairs:
I had rather to adopt a child than get it.—
Come hither, Moor:

Desdemona.   You are the lord of duty,—
I am hitherto your daughter: but here's my husband.
                                    Act I.   Scene III.

I here do give thee that with all my heart
Which, but thou hast already, with all my heart
I would keep from thee.—For your sake, jewel,
I am glad at soul I have no other child;
For thy escape would teach me tyranny,
To hang clogs on them.—I have done, my lord.

DUKE.

Let me speak like yourself; and lay a sentence
Which, as a grise or step, may help these lovers
Into your favor.
When remedies are past, the griefs are ended
By seeing the worst, which late on hopes depended.
To mourn a mischief that is past and gone
Is the next way to draw new mischief on.
What cannot be preserved when fortune takes,
Patience her injury a mockery makes.
The robb'd that smiles steals something from the thief;
He robs himself that spends a bootless grief.

BRABANTIO.

So let the Turk of Cyprus us beguile;
We lose it not so long as we can smile;
He bears the sentence well, that nothing bears
But the free comfort which from thence he hears;
But he bears both the sentence and the sorrow
That, to pay grief, must of poor patience borrow.
These sentences, to sugar or to gall,
Being strong on both sides, are equivocal:
But words are words; I never yet did hear
That the bruis'd heart was pierced through the ear.—
I humbly beseech you, proceed to the affairs of state.

DUKE.

The Turk with a most mighty preparation makes for Cyprus.—
Othello, the fortitude of the place is best known to you; and though
we have there a substitute of most allowed sufficiency, yet opinion,
a sovereign mistress of effects, throws a more safer voice on you:
you must therefore be content to slubber the gloss of your new fortunes with this more stubborn and boisterous expedition.

OTHELLO.

The tyrant custom, most grave senators,
Hath made the flinty and steel couch of war
My thrice-driven bed of down: I do agnize
A natural and prompt alacrity
I find in hardness; and do undertake
These present wars against the Ottomites.
Most humbly, therefore, bending to your state,
I crave fit disposition for my wife;

Due reference of place and exhibition;
With such accommodation and besort
As levels with her breeding.

DUKE.

If you please,
Be't at her father's.

BRABANTIO.

I'll not have it so.

OTHELLO.

Nor I.

DESDEMONA.

Nor I. I would not there reside,
To put my father in impatient thoughts,
By being in his eye. Most gracious duke,
To my unfolding lend your prosperous ear;
And let me find a charter in your voice
To assist my simpleness.

DUKE.

What would you, Desdemona?

DESDEMONA.

That I did love the Moor to live with him,
My downright violence and storm of fortunes
May trumpet to the world: my heart's subdu'd
Even to the very quality of my lord:
I saw Othello's visage in his mind;
And to his honors and his valiant parts
Did I my soul and fortunes consecrate.
So that, dear lords, if I be left behind,
A moth of peace, and he go to the war,
The rites for which I love him are bereft me,
And I a heavy interim shall support
By his dear absence. Let me go with him.

OTHELLO.

Let her have your voices.
Vouch with me, heaven, I therefore beg it not
To please the palate of my appetite;
Nor to comply with heat,—the young affects
In me defunct,—and proper satisfaction;
But to be free and bounteous to her mind:
And heaven defend your good souls, that you think

I will your serious and great business scant
For she is with me: no, when light-wing'd toys
Of feather'd Cupid seel with wanton dullness
My speculative and offic'd instruments,
That my disports corrupt and taint my business,
Let housewives make a skillet of my helm,
And all indign and base adversities
Make head against my estimation!

DUKE.

Be it as you shall privately determine,
Either for her stay or going: the affair cries haste,
And speed must answer it.

FIRST SENATOR.

You must away to-night.

OTHELLO.

With all my heart.

DUKE.

At nine i' the morning here we'll meet again.—
Othello, leave some officer behind,
And he shall our commission bring to you;
With such things else of quality and respect
As doth import you.

OTHELLO.

So please your grace, my ancient,—
A man he is of honesty and trust,—
To his conveyance I assign my wife,
With what else needful your good grace shall think
To be sent after me.

DUKE.

Let it be so.—
Good night to everyone.—*[To* BRABANTIO.*]* And, noble signior,
If virtue no delighted beauty lack,
Your son-in-law is far more fair than black.

FIRST SENATOR.

Adieu, brave Moor; use Desdemona well.

BRABANTIO.

Look to her, Moor, if thou hast eyes to see:
She has deceiv'd her father, and may thee.

[Exeunt DUKE, *Senators, Officers. &c.*

OTHELLO.

My life upon her faith!—Honest Iago,
My Desdemona must I leave to thee:
I pr'ythee, let thy wife attend on her;
And bring them after in the best advantage.—
Come, Desdemona, I have but an hour
Of love, of worldly matters and direction,
To spend with thee: we must obey the time.

[Exeunt OTHELLO *and* DESDEMONA.

Roderigo. I will incontinently drown myself.
Iago. If thou dost, I shall never love thee after.
Why, thou silly gentleman!   *Act I. Scene III.*

RODERIGO.

Iago,—

IAGO.

What say'st thou, noble heart?

RODERIGO.

What will I do, thinkest thou?

IAGO.

Why, go to bed and sleep.

RODERIGO.

I will incontinently drown myself.

IAGO.

If thou dost, I shall never love thee after. Why, thou silly gentleman!

RODERIGO.

It is silliness to live when to live is torment; and then have we a prescription to die when death is our physician.

IAGO.

O villainous! I have looked upon the world for four times seven years, and since I could distinguish betwixt a benefit and an injury, I never found man that knew how to love himself. Ere I would say I would drown myself for the love of a Guinea-hen, I would change my humanity with a baboon.

RODERIGO.

What should I do? I confess it is my shame to be so fond, but it is not in my virtue to amend it.

IAGO.

Virtue! a fig! 'Tis in ourselves that we are thus or thus. Our bodies are gardens, to the which our wills are gardeners; so that if we will plant nettles or sow lettuce, set hyssop and weed up thyme, supply it with one gender of herbs or distract it with many, either to have it sterile with idleness or manured with industry; why, the power and corrigible authority of this lies in our wills. If the balance of our lives had not one scale of reason to poise another of sensuality, the blood and baseness of our natures would conduct us to most preposterous conclusions: But we have reason to cool our raging motions, our carnal stings, our unbitted lusts; whereof I take this, that you call love, to be a sect or scion.

RODERIGO.

It cannot be.

IAGO.

It is merely a lust of the blood and a permission of the will. Come, be a man: drown thyself! drown cats and blind puppies. I have professed me thy friend, and I confess me knit to thy deserving with cables of perdurable toughness; I could never better stead thee than now. Put money in thy purse; follow thou the wars; defeat thy favor with an usurped beard; I say, put money in thy purse. It cannot be that Desdemona should long continue her love to the Moor,—put money in thy purse,—nor he his to her: it was a violent commencement, and thou shalt see an answerable seques-tration;—put but money in thy purse.—These Moors are change-able in their wills:—fill thy purse with money: the food that to him now is as luscious as locusts shall be to him shortly as acerb as the coloquintida. She must change for youth: when she is sated with his body, she will find the error of her choice: she must have change, she must: therefore put money in thy purse.—If thou wilt needs damn thyself, do it a more delicate way than drown-ing. Make all the money thou canst; if sanctimony and a frail vow betwixt an erring barbarian and a supersubtle Venetian be not too hard for my wits and all the tribe of hell, thou shalt enjoy her; therefore make money. A pox of drowning thyself! it is clean out of the way: seek thou rather to be hanged in compassing thy joy than to be drowned and go without her.

RODERIGO.

Wilt thou be fast to my hopes, if I depend on the issue?

IAGO.

Thou art sure of me:—go, make money:—I have told thee often, and I re-tell thee again and again, I hate the Moor: my cause is hearted; thine hath no less reason. Let us be conjunctive in our revenge against him: if thou canst cuckold him, thou dost thyself a pleasure, me a sport. There are many events in the womb of time which will be delivered. Traverse; go; provide thy money. We will have more of this to-morrow. Adieu.

RODERIGO.

Where shall we meet i' the morning?

IAGO.

At my lodging.

RODERIGO.

I'll be with thee betimes.

IAGO.

Go to; farewell. Do you hear, Roderigo?

RODERIGO.

What say you?

IAGO.

No more of drowning, do you hear?

RODERIGO.

I am changed: I'll go sell all my land.

[Exit.

IAGO.

Thus do I ever make my fool my purse;
For I mine own gain'd knowledge should profane
If I would time expend with such a snipe
But for my sport and profit. I hate the Moor;
And it is thought abroad that 'twixt my sheets
He has done my office: I know not if't be true;
But I, for mere suspicion in that kind,
Will do as if for surety. He holds me well,
The better shall my purpose work on him.
Cassio's a proper man: let me see now;
To get his place, and to plume up my will
In double knavery,—How, how?—Let's see:—
After some time, to abuse Othello's ear
That he is too familiar with his wife:—
He hath a person, and a smooth dispose,
To be suspected; fram'd to make women false.
The Moor is of a free and open nature,
That thinks men honest that but seem to be so;
And will as tenderly be led by the nose
As asses are.
I have't;—it is engender'd:—hell and night
Must bring this monstrous birth to the world's light.

[Exit.

ACT II.

SCENE I. *A seaport in Cyprus. A Platform.*

Enter MONTANO *and two* GENTLEMEN.

MONTANO.

What from the cape can you discern at sea?

FIRST GENTLEMAN.

Nothing at all: it is a high-wrought flood;
I cannot, 'twixt the heaven and the main,
Descry a sail.

MONTANO.

Methinks the wind hath spoke aloud at land;
A fuller blast ne'er shook our battlements:
If it hath ruffian'd so upon the sea,
What ribs of oak, when mountains melt on them,
Can hold the mortise? What shall we hear of this?

SECOND GENTLEMAN.

A segregation of the Turkish fleet:
For do but stand upon the foaming shore,
The chidden billow seems to pelt the clouds;
The wind-shak'd surge, with high and monstrous mane,
Seems to cast water on the burning Bear,
And quench the guards of the ever-fixed pole;
I never did like molestation view
On the enchafed flood.

MONTANO.

If that the Turkish fleet
Be not enshelter'd and embay'd, they are drown'd;
It is impossible to bear it out.

Enter a THIRD GENTLEMAN.

THIRD GENTLEMAN.

News, lads! our wars are done.
The desperate tempest hath so bang'd the Turks
That their designment halts; a noble ship of Venice

Hath seen a grievous wreck and sufferance
On most part of their fleet.

MONTANO.

How! is this true?

THIRD GENTLEMAN.

The ship is here put in,
A Veronessa; Michael Cassio,
Lieutenant to the warlike Moor Othello,
Is come on shore: the Moor himself's at sea,
And is in full commission here for Cyprus.

MONTANO.

I am glad on't; 'tis a worthy governor.

THIRD GENTLEMAN.

But this same Cassio,—though he speak of comfort
Touching the Turkish loss,—yet he looks sadly,
And prays the Moor be safe; for they were parted
With foul and violent tempest.

MONTANO.

Pray heavens he be;
For I have serv'd him, and the man commands
Like a full soldier. Let's to the sea-side, ho!
As well to see the vessel that's come in
As to throw out our eyes for brave Othello,
Even till we make the main and the aerial blue
An indistinct regard.

THIRD GENTLEMAN.

Come, let's do so;
For every minute is expectancy
Of more arrivance.

Enter CASSIO.

CASSIO.

Thanks you, the valiant of this warlike isle,
That so approve the Moor! O, let the heavens
Give him defence against the elements,
For I have lost him on a dangerous sea!

MONTANO.

Is he well shipp'd?

CASSIO.

His bark is stoutly timber'd, and his pilot
Of very expert and approv'd allowance;
Therefore my hopes, not surfeited to death,
Stand in bold cure.
[Within.] A sail, a sail, a sail!

Enter a FOURTH GENTLEMAN.

CASSIO.

What noise?

FOURTH GENTLEMAN.

The town is empty; on the brow o' the sea
Stand ranks of people, and they cry, "A sail!"

CASSIO.

My hopes do shape him for the governor.
[Guns within.]

SECOND GENTLEMAN.

They do discharge their shot of courtesy:
Our friends at least.

CASSIO.

I pray you, sir, go forth,
And give us truth who 'tis that is arriv'd.

SECOND GENTLEMAN.

I shall.

[Exit.

MONTANO.

But, good lieutenant, is your general wiv'd?

CASSIO.

Most fortunately: he hath achiev'd a maid
That paragons description and wild fame,
One that excels the quirks of blazoning pens,
And in the essential vesture of creation
Does tire the ingener.—
[Re-enter SECOND GENTLEMAN.*]*
How now! who has put in?

SECOND GENTLEMAN.

'Tis one Iago, ancient to the general.

CASSIO.

He has had most favorable and happy speed:
Tempests themselves, high seas, and howling winds,
The gutter'd rocks, and congregated sands,—
Traitors ensteep'd to clog the guiltless keel,—
As having sense of beauty, do omit
Their mortal natures, letting go safely by
The divine Desdemona.

MONTANO.

What is she?

CASSIO.

She that I spake of, our great captain's captain,
Left in the conduct of the bold Iago;
Whose footing here anticipates our thoughts
A se'nnight's speed.—Great Jove, Othello guard,
And swell his sail with thine own powerful breath,
That he may bless this bay with his tall ship,
Make love's quick pants in Desdemona's arms,
Give renew'd fire to our extincted spirits,
And bring all Cyprus comfort! O, behold,

Enter DESDEMONA, EMILIA, IAGO, RODERIGO, *and Attendants.*

The riches of the ship is come on shore!
Ye men of Cyprus, let her have your knees.—
Hall to thee, lady! and the grace of heaven,
Before, behind thee, and on every hand,
Enwheel thee round!

DESDEMONA.

I thank you, valiant Cassio.
What tidings can you tell me of my lord?

CASSIO.

He is not yet arrived nor know I aught
But that he's well, and will be shortly here.

DESDEMONA.

O, but I fear—How lost you company?

CASSIO.

The great contention of the sea and skies
Parted our fellowship:—but, hark! a sail.
[Within.] A sail, a sail!

[Guns within.]

SECOND GENTLEMAN.

They give their greeting to the citadel:
This likewise is a friend.

CASSIO.

See for the news.

[Exit GENTLEMAN.

Good ancient, you are welcome:—*[To* EMILIA.*]* Welcome, mistress:—
Let it not gall your patience, good Iago,
That I extend my manners; 'tis my breeding
That gives me this bold show of courtesy.
[Kissing her.]

IAGO.

Sir, would she give you so much of her lips
As of her tongue she oft bestows on me,
You'd have enough.

DESDEMONA.

Alas, she has no speech.

IAGO.

In faith, too much;
I find it still when I have list to sleep:
Marry, before your ladyship, I grant,
She puts her tongue a little in her heart,
And chides with thinking.

EMILIA.

You have little cause to say so.

IAGO.

Come on, come on; you are pictures out of doors,
Bells in your parlours, wild cats in your kitchens,
Saints in your injuries, devils being offended,
Players in your housewifery, and housewives in your beds.

DESDEMONA.

O, fie upon thee, slanderer!

IAGO.

Nay, it is true, or else I am a Turk:
You rise to play, and go to bed to work.

EMILIA.

You shall not write my praise.

IAGO.

No, let me not.

DESDEMONA.

What wouldst thou write of me, if thou shouldst praise me?

IAGO.

O gentle lady, do not put me to't;
For I am nothing if not critical.

DESDEMONA.

Come on, assay—There's one gone to the harbor?

IAGO.

Ay, madam.

DESDEMONA.

I am not merry; but I do beguile
The thing I am, by seeming otherwise.—
Come, how wouldst thou praise me?

IAGO.

I am about it; but, indeed, my invention
Comes from my pate as birdlime does from frize,—
It plucks out brains and all: but my Muse labours,
And thus she is deliver'd.
If she be fair and wise,—fairness and wit,
The one's for use, the other useth it.

DESDEMONA.

Well prais'd! How if she be black and witty?

IAGO.

If she be black, and thereto have a wit,
She'll find a white that shall her blackness fit.

DESDEMONA.

Worse and worse.

EMILIA.

How if fair and foolish?

IAGO.

She never yet was foolish that was fair;
For even her folly help'd her to an heir.

DESDEMONA.

These are old fond paradoxes to make fools laugh i' the alehouse.
What miserable praise hast thou for her that's foul and foolish?

IAGO.

There's none so foul and foolish thereunto,
But does foul pranks which fair and wise ones do.

DESDEMONA.

O heavy ignorance!—thou praisest the worst best. But what praise
couldst thou bestow on a deserving woman indeed,—one that, in
the authority of her merit, did justly put on the vouch of very
malice itself?

IAGO.

She that was ever fair and never proud;
Had tongue at will and yet was never loud;
Never lack'd gold and yet went never gay;
Fled from her wish, and yet said, "Now I may";
She that, being anger'd, her revenge being nigh,
Bade her wrong stay and her displeasure fly;
She that in wisdom never was so frail
To change the cod's head for the salmon's tail;
She that could think and ne'er disclose her mind;
See suitors following and not look behind;
She was a wight, if ever such wight were;—

DESDEMONA.

To do what?

IAGO.

To suckle fools and chronicle small beer.

DESDEMONA.

O most lame and impotent conclusion!—Do not learn of him,
Emilia, though he be thy husband.—How say you, Cassio? is he
not a most profane and liberal counsellor?

CASSIO.

He speaks home, madam: you may relish him more in the soldier
than in the scholar.

IAGO.

[Aside.] He takes her by the palm: ay, well said, whisper: with
as little a web as this will I ensnare as great a fly as Cassio. Ay,
smile upon her, do; I will gyve thee in thine own courtship. You

say true; 'tis so, indeed: if such tricks as these strip you out of
your lieutenantry, it had been better you had not kissed your three
fingers so oft, which now again you are most apt to play the sir in.
Very good; well kissed! an excellent courtesy! 'tis so, indeed. Yet
again your fingers to your lips? Would they were clyster-pipes for
your sake!
[Trumpet within.]—The Moor! I know his trumpet.

Othello.   Oh, my fair warrior!
Desdemona.   My dear Othello!
                                                Act II.   Scene I.

CASSIO.

'Tis truly so.

DESDEMONA.

Let's meet him, and receive him.

CASSIO.

Lo, where he comes!

Enter OTHELLO *and Attendants.*

OTHELLO.

O my fair warrior!

DESDEMONA.

My dear Othello!

OTHELLO.

It gives me wonder great as my content
To see you here before me. O my soul's joy!
If after every tempest come such calms,
May the winds blow till they have waken'd death!
And let the laboring bark climb hills of seas
Olympus-high, and duck again as low
As hell's from heaven! If it were now to die,
'Twere now to be most happy; for, I fear,
My soul hath her content so absolute
That not another comfort like to this
Succeeds in unknown fate.

DESDEMONA.

The heavens forbid
But that our loves and comforts should increase
Even as our days do grow!

OTHELLO.

Amen to that, sweet powers!—
I cannot speak enough of this content;
It stops me here; it is too much of joy:
And this, and this, the greatest discords be
[Kissing her.]
That e'er our hearts shall make!

IAGO.

[Aside.] O, you are well tun'd now!
But I'll set down the pegs that make this music,
As honest as I am.

OTHELLO.

Come, let us to the castle.—
News, friends; our wars are done, the Turks are drown'd.
How does my old acquaintance of this isle?
Honey, you shall be well desir'd in Cyprus;
I have found great love amongst them. O my sweet,
I prattle out of fashion, and I dote
In mine own comforts.—I pry'thee, good Iago,
Go to the bay and disembark my coffers:
Bring thou the master to the citadel;
He is a good one, and his worthiness
Does challenge much respect.—Come, Desdemona,
Once more well met at Cyprus.

[Exeunt OTHELLO, DESDEMONA, *and Attendants.*

IAGO.

Do thou meet me presently at the harbor. Come hither. If thou
be'st valiant,—as, they say, base men being in love have then a
nobility in their natures more than is native to them,—list me. The
lieutenant to-night watches on the court of guard: first, I must tell
thee this—Desdemona is directly in love with him.

RODERIGO.

With him! why, 'tis not possible.

IAGO.

Lay thy finger thus, and let thy soul be instructed. Mark me with
what violence she first loved the Moor, but for bragging, and tell-
ing her fantastical lies: and will she love him still for prating? Let
not thy discreet heart think it. Her eye must be fed; and what delight shall she have to look on the devil? When the blood is made
dull with the act of sport, there should be,—again to inflame it and
to give satiety a fresh appetite,— loveliness in favor; sympathy in
years, manners, and beauties; all which the Moor is defective in:
now, for want of these required conveniences, her delicate tender-
ness will find itself abused, begin to heave the gorge, disrelish and
abhor the Moor; very nature will instruct her in it, and compel her
to some second choice. Now sir, this granted;—as it is a most preg-
nant and unforced position,—who stands so eminently in the degree of this fortune as Cassio does? a knave very voluble; no further
conscionable than in putting on the mere form of civil and humane
seeming, for the better compass of his salt and most hidden loose

affection? why, none; why, none;—a slipper and subtle knave; a
finder out of occasions; that has an eye can stamp and counterfeit
advantages, though true advantage never present itself: a devilish
knave! besides, the knave is handsome, young, and hath all those
requisites in him that folly and green minds look after: a pestilent
complete knave; and the woman hath found him already.

Roderigo.

I cannot believe that in her; she is full of most blessed condition.

Iago.

Blest fig's end! the wine she drinks is made of grapes: if she had
been blessed, she would never have loved the Moor: blessed pud-
ding! Didst thou not see her paddle with the palm of his hand?
didst not mark that?

Roderigo.

Yes, that I did; but that was but courtesy.

Iago.

Lechery, by this hand; an index and obscure prologue to the history of lust and foul thoughts. They met so near with their lips that
their breaths embraced together. Villainous thoughts, Roderigo!
when these mutualities so marshal the way, hard at hand comes
the master and main exercise, the incorporate conclusion: pish!—
But, sir, be you ruled by me: I have brought you from Venice.
Watch you to-night: for the command, I'll lay't upon you: Cassio
knows you not:—I'll not be far from you: do you find some occasion to anger Cassio, either by speaking too loud, or tainting his
discipline, or from what other course you please, which the time
shall more favorably minister.

Roderigo.

Well.

Iago.

Sir, he is rash, and very sudden in choler, and haply strike at you:
provoke him, that he may; for even out of that will I cause these
of Cyprus to mutiny, whose qualification shall come into no true
taste again but by the displanting of Cassio. So shall you have a
shorter journey to your desires by the means I shall then have to
prefer them; and the impediment most profitably removed, without the which there were no expectation of our prosperity.

RODERIGO.

I will do this, if I can bring it to any opportunity.

IAGO.

I warrant thee. Meet me by and by at the citadel: I must fetch his necessaries ashore. Farewell.

RODERIGO.

Adieu.

[Exit.

IAGO.

That Cassio loves her, I do well believe it;
That she loves him, 'tis apt, and of great credit:
The Moor,—howbeit that I endure him not,—
Is of a constant, loving, noble nature;
And, I dare think, he'll prove to Desdemona
A most dear husband. Now, I do love her too;
Not out of absolute lust,—though, peradventure,
I stand accountant for as great a sin,—
But partly led to diet my revenge,
For that I do suspect the lusty Moor
Hath leap'd into my seat: the thought whereof
Doth, like a poisonous mineral, gnaw my inwards;
And nothing can or shall content my soul
Till I am even'd with him, wife for wife;
Or, failing so, yet that I put the Moor
At least into a jealousy so strong
That judgement cannot cure. Which thing to do,—
If this poor trash of Venice, whom I trash
For his quick hunting, stand the putting on,
I'll have our Michael Cassio on the hip;
Abuse him to the Moor in the rank garb,—
For I fear Cassio with my night-cap too;—
Make the Moor thank me, love me, and reward me
For making him egregiously an ass
And practicing upon his peace and quiet
Even to madness. 'Tis here, but yet confus'd:
Knavery's plain face is never seen till us'd.

[Exit.

SCENE II. *A street.*

Enter a HERALD *with a proclamation; People following.*

HERALD.

It is Othello's pleasure, our noble and valiant general, that upon certain tidings now arrived, importing the mere perdition of the Turkish fleet, every man put himself into triumph; some to dance, some to make bonfires, each man to what sport and revels his addiction leads him: for, besides these beneficial news, it is the celebration of his nuptial:—so much was his pleasure should be proclaimed. All offices are open; and there is full liberty of feasting from this present hour of five till the bell have told eleven. Heaven bless the isle of Cyprus and our noble general Othello!

[Exeunt.

SCENE III. *A Hall in the Castle.*

Enter OTHELLO, DESDEMONA, CASSIO, *and Attendants.*

OTHELLO.

Good Michael, look you to the guard to-night:
Let's teach ourselves that honorable stop,
Not to out-sport discretion.

CASSIO.

Iago hath direction what to do;
But, notwithstanding, with my personal eye
Will I look to't.

OTHELLO.

Iago is most honest.
Michael, good night: to-morrow with your earliest
Let me have speech with you.—*[To* DESDEMONA*]* Come, my dear love,—
The purchase made, the fruits are to ensue;
That profit's yet to come 'tween me and you.—
Good-night.

[Exeunt OTHELLO, DESDEMONA, *and Attendants.*

Enter IAGO.

CASSIO.

Welcome, Iago; we must to the watch.

IAGO.

Not this hour, lieutenant; 'tis not yet ten o' the clock. Our general cast us thus early for the love of his Desdemona; who let us not therefore blame: he hath not yet made wanton the night with her; and she is sport for Jove.

CASSIO.

She's a most exquisite lady.

IAGO.

And, I'll warrant her, full of game.

CASSIO.

Indeed, she is a most fresh and delicate creature.

IAGO.

What an eye she has! methinks it sounds a parley to provocation.

CASSIO.

An inviting eye; and yet methinks right modest.

IAGO.

And when she speaks, is it not an alarm to love?

CASSIO.

She is, indeed, perfection.

IAGO.

Well, happiness to their sheets! Come, lieutenant, I have a stoop of wine; and here without are a brace of Cyprus gallants that would fain have a measure to the health of black Othello.

CASSIO.

Not to-night, good Iago: I have very poor and unhappy brains for drinking: I could well wish courtesy would invent some other custom of entertainment.

IAGO.

O, they are our friends; but one cup: I'll drink for you.

CASSIO.

I have drunk but one cup to-night, and that was craftily qualified too, and behold, what innovation it makes here: I am unfortunate in the infirmity, and dare not task my weakness with any more.

IAGO.

What, man! 'tis a night of revels: the gallants desire it.

CASSIO.

Where are they?

IAGO.

Here at the door; I pray you, call them in.

CASSIO.

I'll do't; but it dislikes me.

[Exit.

IAGO.

If I can fasten but one cup upon him,
With that which he hath drunk to-night already,
He'll be as full of quarrel and offense
As my young mistress' dog. Now, my sick fool Roderigo,
Whom love hath turn'd almost the wrong side out,
To Desdemona hath to-night carous'd
Potations pottle-deep; and he's to watch:
Three lads of Cyprus,—noble swelling spirits,
That hold their honors in a wary distance,
The very elements of this warlike isle,—
Have I to-night fluster'd with flowing cups,
And they watch too. Now, 'mongst this flock of drunkards,
Am I to put our Cassio in some action
That may offend the isle:—but here they come:
If consequence do but approve my dream,
My boat sails freely, both with wind and stream.
[Re-enter Cassio; with him Montano and Gentlemen; followed by
Servant with wine.]

CASSIO.

'Fore heaven, they have given me a rouse already.

MONTANO.

Good faith, a little one; not past a pint, as I am a soldier.

IAGO.

Some wine, ho!
[Sings.]

> "And let me the canakin clink, clink;
> And let me the canakin clink.
>   A soldier's a man;
>   O, man's life's but a span;
> Why then let a soldier drink."

Some wine, boys!

CASSIO.

'Fore God, an excellent song.

IAGO.

I learned it in England, where, indeed, they are most potent in potting: your Dane, your German, and your swag-bellied Hollander,—Drink, ho!—are nothing to your English.

CASSIO.

Is your Englishman so expert in his drinking?

IAGO.

Why, he drinks you, with facility, your Dane dead drunk; he sweats not to overthrow your Almain; he gives your Hollander a vomit ere the next pottle can be filled.

CASSIO.

To the health of our general!

MONTANO.

I am for it, lieutenant; and I'll do you justice.

IAGO.

O sweet England!

[Sings.]

> "King Stephen was and a worthy peer,
>   His breeches cost him but a crown;
> He held them sixpence all too dear,
>   With that he call'd the tailor lown.
> He was a wight of high renown,
>   And thou art but of low degree:
> 'Tis pride that pulls the country down;
>   Then take thine auld cloak about thee."

Some wine, ho!

CASSIO.

Why, this is a more exquisite song than the other.

IAGO.

Will you hear it again?

CASSIO.

No; for I hold him to be unworthy of his place that does those things.—Well,—God's above all, and there be souls must be saved, and there be souls must not be saved.

IAGO.

It's true, good lieutenant.

Cassio.

For mine own part,—no offence to the general, nor any man of quality,—I hope to be saved.

Iago.

And so do I too, lieutenant.

Cassio.

Ay, but, by your leave, not before me; the lieutenant is to be saved before the ancient. Let's have no more of this; let's to our affairs.— Forgive us our sins!—Gentlemen, let's look to our business. Do not think, gentlemen, I am drunk: this is my ancient; this is my right hand, and this is my left:—I am not drunk now; I can stand well enough, and I speak well enough.

All.

Excellent well.

Cassio.

Why, very well then: you must not think, then, that I am drunk.

[Exit.

Montano.

To the platform, masters; come, let's set the watch.

Iago.

You see this fellow that is gone before;—
He is a soldier fit to stand by Caesar
And give direction: and do but see his vice;
'Tis to his virtue a just equinox,
The one as long as the other: 'tis pity of him.
I fear the trust Othello puts him in,
On some odd time of his infirmity,
Will shake this island.

Montano.

But is he often thus?

Iago.

'Tis evermore the prologue to his sleep:
He'll watch the horologe a double set
If drink rock not his cradle.

Montano.

It were well
The general were put in mind of it.

Perhaps he sees it not, or his good nature
Prizes the virtue that appears in Cassio,
And looks not on his evils: is not this true?

Enter RODERIGO.

IAGO.

[Aside to him.] How now, Roderigo!
I pray you, after the lieutenant; go.

[Exit RODERIGO.

MONTANO.

And 'tis great pity that the noble Moor
Should hazard such a place as his own second
With one of an ingraft infirmity:
It were an honest action to say
So to the Moor.

IAGO.

Not I, for this fair island;
I do love Cassio well; and would do much
To cure him of this evil.—But, hark! What noise?
[Cry within,—"Help! help!"]

[Re-enter CASSIO, *driving in* RODERIGO.]*

CASSIO.

You rogue! you rascal!

MONTANO.

What's the matter, lieutenant?

CASSIO.

A knave teach me my duty! I'll beat the knave into a twiggen
bottle.

RODERIGO.

Beat me!

CASSIO.

Dost thou prate, rogue? *[Striking* RODERIGO.]*

MONTANO.

Nay, good lieutenant; I pray you, sir, hold your hand.

CASSIO.

Let me go, sir, or I'll knock you o'er the mazard.

MONTANO.

Come, come, you're drunk.

CASSIO.

Drunk!

[They fight.]

IAGO.

[Aside to RODERIGO.*]* Away, I say! go out and cry a mutiny.
[Exit RODERIGO.*]*
Nay, good lieutenant,—alas,, gentlemen:—
Help, ho!—Lieutenant,—sir,—Montano,—sir:—
Help, masters!—Here's a goodly watch indeed!
[Bell rings.]
Who's that that rings the bell?—Diablo, ho!
The town will rise: God's will, lieutenant, hold;
You will be sham'd forever.

[Re-enter OTHELLO *and Attendants.]*

OTHELLO.

What is the matter here?

MONTANO.

Zounds, I bleed still; I am hurt to the death.

OTHELLO.

Hold, for your lives!

IAGO.

Hold, ho! lieutenant,—sir,—Montano,—gentlemen,—
Have you forgot all sense of place and duty?
Hold! the general speaks to you; hold, hold, for shame!

OTHELLO.

Why, how now, ho! from whence ariseth this?
Are we turn'd Turks, and to ourselves do that
Which Heaven hath forbid the Ottomites?
For Christian shame, put by this barbarous brawl:
He that stirs next to carve for his own rage
Holds his soul light; he dies upon his motion.—
Silence that dreadful bell; it frights the isle
From her propriety.—What is the matter, masters?—
Honest Iago, that look'st dead with grieving,
Speak, who began this? on thy love, I charge thee.

IAGO.

I do not know:—friends all but now, even now,
In quarter, and in terms like bride and groom
Devesting them for bed; and then, but now—
As if some planet had unwitted men,—
Swords out, and tilting one at other's breast
In opposition bloody. I cannot speak
Any beginning to this peevish odds;
And would in action glorious I had lost
Those legs that brought me to a part of it!

OTHELLO.

How comes it, Michael, you are thus forgot?

CASSIO.

I pray you, pardon me; I cannot speak.

OTHELLO.

Worthy Montano, you were wont be civil;
The gravity and stillness of your youth
The world hath noted, and your name is great
In mouths of wisest censure: what's the matter,
That you unlace your reputation thus,
And spend your rich opinion for the name
Of a night-brawler? give me answer to it.

MONTANO.

Worthy Othello, I am hurt to danger:
Your officer, Iago, can inform you,—
While I spare speech, which something now offends me,—
Of all that I do know: nor know I aught
By me that's said or done amiss this night:
Unless self-charity be sometimes a vice,
And to defend ourselves it be a sin
When violence assails us.

OTHELLO.

Now, by heaven,
My blood begins my safer guides to rule;
And passion, having my best judgement collied,
Assays to lead the way. If I once stir,
Or do but lift this arm, the best of you
Shall sink in my rebuke. Give me to know
How this foul rout began, who set it on;

And he that is approv'd in this offense,
Though he had twinn'd with me, both at a birth,
Shall lose me.—What! in a town of war
Yet wild, the people's hearts brimful of fear,
To manage private and domestic quarrel,
In night, and on the court and guard of safety!
'Tis monstrous.—Iago, who began't?

MONTANO.

If partially affin'd, or leagu'd in office,
Thou dost deliver more or less than truth,
Thou art no soldier.

IAGO.

Touch me not so near:
I had rather have this tongue cut from my mouth
Than it should do offence to Michael Cassio;
Yet, I persuade myself, to speak the truth
Shall nothing wrong him.—Thus it is, general.
Montano and myself being in speech,
There comes a fellow crying out for help;
And Cassio following him with determin'd sword,
To execute upon him. Sir, this gentleman
Steps in to Cassio and entreats his pause:
Myself the crying fellow did pursue,
Lest by his clamor,—as it so fell out,—
The town might fall in fright: he, swift of foot,
Outran my purpose; and I return'd the rather
For that I heard the clink and fall of swords,
And Cassio high in oath; which till to-night
I ne'er might say before. When I came back,—
For this was brief,—I found them close together,
At blow and thrust; even as again they were
When you yourself did part them.
More of this matter cannot I report;—
But men are men; the best sometimes forget:—
Though Cassio did some little wrong to him,—
As men in rage strike those that wish them best,—
Yet surely Cassio, I believe, receiv'd
From him that fled some strange indignity,
Which patience could not pass.

OTHELLO.

I know, Iago,
Thy honesty and love doth mince this matter,
Making it light to Cassio. Cassio, I love thee;
But never more be officer of mine.—

[Re-enter DESDEMONA, *attended.]*

Look, if my gentle love be not rais'd up!—
I'll make thee an example.

DESDEMONA.

What's the matter?

OTHELLO.

All's well now, sweeting; come away to bed.

[To MONTANO, *who is led off.]*

Sir, for your hurts, myself will be your surgeon:
Lead him off.
Iago, look with care about the town,
And silence those whom this vile brawl distracted.—
Come, Desdemona: 'tis the soldiers' life
To have their balmy slumbers wak'd with strife.

[Exeunt all but IAGO *and* CASSIO.

IAGO.

What, are you hurt, lieutenant?

CASSIO.

Ay, past all surgery.

IAGO.

Marry, heaven forbid!

CASSIO.

Reputation, reputation, reputation! O, I have lost my reputation!
I have lost the immortal part of myself, and what remains is bes-
tial.—My reputation, Iago, my reputation!

IAGO.

As I am an honest man, I thought you had received some bodily
wound; there is more sense in that than in reputation. Reputation
is an idle and most false imposition; oft got without merit and lost
without deserving: you have lost no reputation at all, unless you
repute yourself such a loser. What, man! there are ways to recover
the general again: you are but now cast in his mood, a punishment

more in policy than in malice; even so as one would beat his of-fenceless dog to affright an imperious lion: sue to him again, and he is yours.

Iago. What! are you hurt, lieutenant?
Cassio. Ay, past all surgery.
Iago. Marry, Heaven forbid! *Act II. Scene III.*

CASSIO.

I will rather sue to be despised than to deceive so good a command-er with so slight, so drunken, and so indiscreet an officer. Drunk? and speak parrot? and squabble? swagger? swear? and discourse fustian with one's own shadow?—O thou invisible spirit of wine, if thou hast no name to be known by, let us call thee devil!

IAGO.

What was he that you followed with your sword? What had he done to you?

CASSIO.

I know not.

IAGO.

Is't possible?

CASSIO.

I remember a mass of things, but nothing distinctly; a quarrel, but nothing wherefore.—O God, that men should put an enemy in their mouths to steal away their brains! that we should, with joy, pleasance, revel, and applause, transform ourselves into beasts!

IAGO.

Why, but you are now well enough: how came you thus recovered?

CASSIO.

It hath pleased the devil drunkenness to give place to the devil wrath: one unperfectness shows me another, to make me frankly despise myself.

IAGO.

Come, you are too severe a moraler: as the time, the place, and the condition of this country stands, I could heartily wish this had not befallen; but since it is as it is, mend it for your own good.

CASSIO.

I will ask him for my place again;—he shall tell me I am a drunkard! Had I as many mouths as Hydra, such an answer would stop them all. To be now a sensible man, by and by a fool, and presently a beast! O strange!—Every inordinate cup is unbless'd, and the ingredient is a devil.

IAGO.

Come, come, good wine is a good familiar creature, if it be well used: exclaim no more against it. And, good lieutenant, I think you think I love you.

CASSIO.

I have well approved it, sir.—I drunk!

IAGO.

You, or any man living, may be drunk at a time, man. I'll tell you what you shall do. Our general's wife is now the general;— I may say so in this respect, for that he hath devoted and given up himself to the contemplation, mark, and denotement of her parts and graces:—confess yourself freely to her; importune her help to put you in your place again: she is of so free, so kind, so apt, so blessed a disposition, she holds it a vice in her goodness not to do more than she is requested: this broken joint between you and her husband entreat her to splinter; and, my fortunes against any lay worth naming, this crack of your love shall grow stronger than it was before.

CASSIO.

You advise me well.

IAGO.

I protest, in the sincerity of love and honest kindness.

CASSIO.

I think it freely; and betimes in the morning I will beseech the virtuous Desdemona to undertake for me; I am desperate of my fortunes if they check me here.

IAGO.

You are in the right. Good-night, lieutenant; I must to the watch.

CASSIO.

Good night, honest Iago.

[Exit.

IAGO.

And what's he, then, that says I play the villain?
When this advice is free I give and honest,
Probal to thinking, and, indeed, the course
To win the Moor again? For 'tis most easy
The inclining Desdemona to subdue
In any honest suit: she's fram'd as fruitful
As the free elements. And then for her
To win the Moor,—were't to renounce his baptism,
All seals and symbols of redeemed sin,—
His soul is so enfetter'd to her love
That she may make, unmake, do what she list,
Even as her appetite shall play the god
With his weak function. How am I, then, a villain
To counsel Cassio to this parallel course,
Directly to his good? Divinity of hell!
When devils will the blackest sins put on,
They do suggest at first with heavenly shows,
As I do now: for whiles this honest fool
Plies Desdemona to repair his fortune,
And she for him pleads strongly to the Moor,
I'll pour this pestilence into his ear,—
That she repeals him for her body's lust;
And by how much she strives to do him good,
She shall undo her credit with the Moor.
So will I turn her virtue into pitch;
And out of her own goodness make the net
That shall enmesh them all.

Enter RODERIGO.

How now, Roderigo!

RODERIGO.

I do follow here in the chase, not like a hound that hunts, but one that fills up the cry. My money is almost spent; I have been to-night exceedingly well cudgelled; and I think the issue will be—I shall have so much experience for my pains: and so, with no money at all and a little more wit, return again to Venice.

IAGO.

How poor are they that have not patience!
What wound did ever heal but by degrees?
Thou know'st we work by wit, and not by witchcraft;
And wit depends on dilatory time.
Does't not go well? Cassio hath beaten thee,
And thou, by that small hurt, hast cashier'd Cassio;
Though other things grow fair against the sun,
Yet fruits that blossom first will first be ripe:
Content thyself awhile.—By the mass, 'tis morning;
Pleasure and action make the hours seem short.—
Retire thee; go where thou art billeted:
Away, I say; thou shalt know more hereafter;
Nay, get thee gone.

[Exit RODERIGO.

Two things are to be done,—
My wife must move for Cassio to her mistress;
I'll set her on;
Myself the while to draw the Moor apart,
And bring him jump when he may Cassio find
Soliciting his wife. Ay, that's the way;
Dull not device by coldness and delay.

[Exit.

ACT III.

SCENE I. *Cyprus. Before the Castle.*

Enter Cassio *and some Musicians.*

Cassio.

Masters, play here,—I will content your pains,
Something that's brief; and bid "Good-morrow, general."
[*Music.*]

Enter Clown.

Clown.

Why, masters, have your instruments been in Naples, that they
speak i' the nose thus?

First Musician.

How, sir, how!

Clown.

Are these, I pray you, wind instruments?

First Musician.

Ay, marry, are they, sir.

Clown.

O, thereby hangs a tale.

First Musician.

Whereby hangs a tale, sir?

Clown.

Marry, sir, by many a wind instrument that I know. But, masters,
here's money for you: and the general so likes your music, that he
desires you, for love's sake, to make no more noise with it.

First Musician.

Well, sir, we will not.

Clown.

If you have any music that may not be heard, to't again: but, as
they say, to hear music the general does not greatly care.

First Musician.

We have none such, sir.

CLOWN.

Then put up your pipes in your bag, for I'll away: go, vanish into
air, away!

[Exeunt MUSICIANS.

CASSIO.

Dost thou hear, mine honest friend?

CLOWN.

No, I hear not your honest friend; I hear you.

CASSIO.

Pr'ythee, keep up thy quillets. There's a poor piece of gold for
thee: if the gentlewoman that attends the general's wife be stirring, tell her there's one Cassio entreats her a little favor of speech:
wilt thou do this?

CLOWN.

She is stirring, sir; if she will stir hither I shall seem to notify unto
her.

CASSIO.

Do, good my friend.

[Exit CLOWN.

Enter IAGO.

In happy time, Iago.

IAGO.

You have not been a-bed, then?

CASSIO.

Why, no; the day had broke
Before we parted. I have made bold, Iago,
To send in to your wife: my suit to her
Is, that she will to virtuous Desdemona
Procure me some access.

IAGO.

I'll send her to you presently;
And I'll devise a mean to draw the Moor
Out of the way, that your converse and business
May be more free.

CASSIO.

I humbly thank you for't.   *[Exit* IAGO.*]*
I never knew
A Florentine more kind and honest.

Enter EMILIA.

EMILIA.

Good-morrow, good lieutenant; I am sorry
For your displeasure; but all will sure be well.
The general and his wife are talking of it;
And she speaks for you stoutly: the Moor replies
That he you hurt is of great fame in Cyprus
And great affinity, and that, in wholesome wisdom,
He might not but refuse you; but he protests he loves you
And needs no other suitor but his likings
To take the safest occasion by the front
To bring you in again.

CASSIO.

Yet, I beseech you,—
If you think fit, or that it may be done,—
Give me advantage of some brief discourse
With Desdemona alone.

EMILIA.

Pray you, come in:
I will bestow you where you shall have time
To speak your bosom freely.

CASSIO.

I am much bound to you.

[Exeunt.

SCENE II. *Cyprus. A Room in the Castle.*

Enter OTHELLO, IAGO, *and* GENTLEMEN.

OTHELLO.

These letters give, Iago, to the pilot;
And by him do my duties to the senate:
That done, I will be walking on the works;
Repair there to me.

IAGO.

Well, my good lord, I'll do't.

OTHELLO.

This fortification, gentlemen,—shall we see't?

GENTLEMEN.

We'll wait upon your lordship.

[Exeunt.

SCENE III. *Cyprus. The Garden of the Castle.*

Enter DESDEMONA, CASSIO, *and* EMILIA.

DESDEMONA.

Be thou assured, good Cassio, I will do
All my abilities in thy behalf.

EMILIA.

Good madam, do: I warrant it grieves my husband
As if the cause were his.

DESDEMONA.

O, that's an honest fellow.—Do not doubt, Cassio,
But I will have my lord and you again
As friendly as you were.

CASSIO.

Bounteous madam,
Whatever shall become of Michael Cassio,
He's never anything but your true servant.

DESDEMONA.

I know't,—I thank you. You do love my lord:
You have known him long; and be you well assur'd
He shall in strangeness stand no farther off
Than in a politic distance.

CASSIO.

Ay, but, lady,
That policy may either last so long,
Or feed upon such nice and waterish diet,
Or breed itself so out of circumstance,
That, I being absent, and my place supplied,
My general will forget my love and service.

DESDEMONA.

Do not doubt that; before Emilia here
I give thee warrant of thy place: assure thee,
If I do vow a friendship, I'll perform it
To the last article: my lord shall never rest;
I'll watch him tame, and talk him out of patience;

His bed shall seem a school, his board a shrift;
I'll intermingle everything he does
With Cassio's suit: therefore be merry, Cassio;
For thy solicitor shall rather die
Than give thy cause away.

Cassio.   Bounteous madam,
Whatever shall become of Michael Cassio,
He's never anything but your true servant.   *Act III.   Scene III.*

EMILIA.
Madam, here comes my lord.

CASSIO.
Madam, I'll take my leave.

DESDEMONA.
Why, stay, and hear me speak.

CASSIO.
Madam, not now. I am very ill at ease,
Unfit for mine own purposes.

DESDEMONA.
Well, do your discretion.

[Exit CASSIO.

Enter OTHELLO *and* IAGO.

IAGO.

Ha! I like not that.

OTHELLO.

What dost thou say?

IAGO.

Nothing, my lord: or if—I know not what.

OTHELLO.

Was not that Cassio parted from my wife?

IAGO.

Cassio, my lord! No, sure, I cannot think it,
That he would steal away so guilty-like,
Seeing you coming.

OTHELLO.

I do believe 'twas he.

DESDEMONA.

How now, my lord!
I have been talking with a suitor here,
A man that languishes in your displeasure.

OTHELLO.

Who is't you mean?

DESDEMONA.

Why, your lieutenant, Cassio. Good my lord,
If I have any grace or power to move you,
His present reconciliation take;
For if he be not one that truly loves you,
That errs in ignorance and not in cunning,
I have no judgement in an honest face:
I pr'ythee, call him back.

OTHELLO.

Went he hence now?

DESDEMONA.

Ay, sooth; so humbled
That he hath left part of his grief with me
To suffer with him. Good love, call him back.

OTHELLO.

Not now, sweet Desdemon; some other time.

DESDEMONA.

But shall't be shortly?

OTHELLO.

The sooner, sweet, for you.

DESDEMONA.

Shall't be to-night at supper?

OTHELLO.

No, not to-night.

DESDEMONA.

To-morrow dinner then?

OTHELLO.

I shall not dine at home;
I meet the captains at the citadel.

DESDEMONA.

Why then to-morrow night; or Tuesday morn;
On Tuesday noon, or night; on Wednesday morn:—
I pr'ythee, name the time; but let it not
Exceed three days: in faith, he's penitent;
And yet his trespass, in our common reason,—
Save that, they say, the wars must make examples
Out of their best,—is not almost a fault
To incur a private check. When shall he come?
Tell me, Othello: I wonder in my soul,
What you would ask me, that I should deny,
Or stand so mammering on. What! Michael Cassio,
That came awooing with you; and so many a time,
When I have spoke of you dispraisingly,
Hath ta'en your part;—to have so much to do
To bring him in! Trust me, I could do much,—

OTHELLO.

Pr'ythee, no more; let him come when he will;
I will deny thee nothing.

DESDEMONA.

Why, this is not a boon;
'Tis as I should entreat you wear your gloves,
Or feed on nourishing dishes, or keep you warm,
Or sue to you to do a peculiar profit
To your own person: nay, when I have a suit

Wherein I mean to touch your love indeed,
It shall be full of poise and difficult weight,
And fearful to be granted.

OTHELLO.

I will deny thee nothing:
Whereon, I do beseech thee, grant me this,
To leave me but a little to myself.

DESDEMONA.

Shall I deny you? no: farewell, my lord.

OTHELLO.

Farewell, my Desdemona: I'll come to thee straight.

DESDEMONA.

Emilia, come.—Be as your fancies teach you;
Whate'er you be, I am obedient.

[Exit with EMILIA.

OTHELLO.

Excellent wretch! Perdition catch my soul,
But I do love thee! and when I love thee not,
Chaos is come again.

IAGO.

My noble lord,—

OTHELLO.

What dost thou say, Iago?

IAGO.

Did Michael Cassio, when you woo'd my lady,
Know of your love?

OTHELLO.

He did, from first to last: why dost thou ask?

IAGO.

But for a satisfaction of my thought;
No further harm.

OTHELLO.

Why of thy thought, Iago?

IAGO.

I did not think he had been acquainted with her.

OTHELLO.

O, yes; and went between us very oft.

IAGO.

Indeed!

OTHELLO.

Indeed! ay, indeed:—discern'st thou aught in that?
Is he not honest?

IAGO.

Honest, my lord!

OTHELLO.

Honest! ay, honest.

IAGO.

My lord, for aught I know.

OTHELLO.

What dost thou think?

IAGO.

Think, my lord!

OTHELLO.

Think, my lord! By heaven, he echoes me,
As if there were some monster in his thought
Too hideous to be shown.—Thou dost mean something:
I heard thee say even now,—thou lik'dst not that,
When Cassio left my wife. What didst not like?
And when I told thee he was of my counsel
In my whole course of wooing, thou criedst, "Indeed!"
And didst contract and purse thy brow together,
As if thou then hadst shut up in thy brain
Some horrible conceit: if thou dost love me,
Show me thy thought.

IAGO.

My lord, you know I love you.

OTHELLO.

I think thou dost;
And,—for I know thou'rt full of love and honesty
And weigh'st thy words before thou giv'st them breath,—
Therefore these stops of thine fright me the more:
For such things in a false disloyal knave
Are tricks of custom; but in a man that's just
They're close delations, working from the heart,
That passion cannot rule.

Iago.

For Michael Cassio,
I dare be sworn I think that he is honest.

Othello.

I think so too.

Iago.

Men should be what they seem;
Or those that be not, would they might seem none!

Othello.

Certain, men should be what they seem.

Iago.

Why, then, I think Cassio's an honest man.

Othello.

Nay, yet there's more in this:
I pr'ythee, speak to me as to thy thinkings,
As thou dost ruminate; and give thy worst of thoughts
The worst of words.

Iago.

Good my lord, pardon me:
Though I am bound to every act of duty,
I am not bound to that all slaves are free to.
Utter my thoughts? Why, say they are vile and false;—
As where's that palace whereinto foul things
Sometimes intrude not? who has a breast so pure
But some uncleanly apprehensions
Keep leets and law-days, and in session sit
With meditations lawful?

Othello.

Thou dost conspire against thy friend, Iago,
If thou but think'st him wrong'd and mak'st his ear
A stranger to thy thoughts.

Iago.

I do beseech you,—
Though I perchance am vicious in my guess,
As, I confess, it is my nature's plague
To spy into abuses, and of my jealousy
Shape faults that are not,—that your wisdom yet,
From one that so imperfectly conceits,

Would take no notice; nor build yourself a trouble
Out of his scattering and unsure observance:—
It were not for your quiet nor your good,
Nor for my manhood, honesty, or wisdom,
To let you know my thoughts.

OTHELLO.

What dost thou mean?

IAGO.

Good name in man and woman, dear my lord,
Is the immediate jewel of their souls:
Who steals my purse steals trash; 'tis something, nothing;
'Twas mine, 'tis his, and has been slave to thousands;
But he that filches from me my good name
Robs me of that which not enriches him
And makes me poor indeed.

OTHELLO.

By heaven, I'll know thy thoughts.

IAGO.

You cannot, if my heart were in your hand;
Nor shall not, whilst 'tis in my custody.

OTHELLO.

Ha!

IAGO.

O, beware, my lord, of jealousy;
It is the green-ey'd monster which doth mock
The meat it feeds on: that cuckold lives in bliss
Who, certain of his fate, loves not his wronger;
But O, what damned minutes tells he o'er
Who dotes, yet doubts, suspects, yet strongly loves!

OTHELLO.

O misery!

IAGO.

Poor and content is rich, and rich enough;
But riches fineless is as poor as winter
To him that ever fears he shall be poor;—
Good heaven, the souls of all my tribe defend
From jealousy!

OTHELLO.

Why, why is this?
Think'st thou I'd make a life of jealousy,
To follow still the changes of the moon
With fresh suspicions? No; to be once in doubt
Is once to be resolv'd: exchange me for a goat
When I shall turn the business of my soul
To such exsufflicate and blown surmises,
Matching thy inference. 'Tis not to make me jealous,
To say my wife is fair, feeds well, loves company,
Is free of speech, sings, plays, and dances well;
Where virtue is, these are more virtuous:
Nor from mine own weak merits will I draw
The smallest fear or doubt of her revolt;
For she had eyes and chose me. No, Iago;
I'll see before I doubt; when I doubt, prove;
And on the proof, there is no more but this,—
Away at once with love or jealousy!

IAGO.

I am glad of it; for now I shall have reason
To show the love and duty that I bear you
With franker spirit: therefore, as I am bound,
Receive it from me:—I speak not yet of proof.
Look to your wife; observe her well with Cassio;
Wear your eye thus, not jealous nor secure:
I would not have your free and noble nature,
Out of self-bounty, be abus'd; look to't.
I know our country disposition well;
In Venice they do let heaven see the pranks
They dare not show their husbands; their best conscience
Is not to leave undone, but keep unknown.

OTHELLO.

Dost thou say so?

IAGO.

She did deceive her father, marrying you;
And when she seem'd to shake and fear your looks,
She loved them most.

OTHELLO.

And so she did.

Iago. Look to your wife; observe her well with Cassio.
Act III. Scene III.

IAGO.

Why, go to then;
She that, so young, could give out such a seeming,
To seal her father's eyes up close as oak,—
He thought 'twas witchcraft,—but I am much to blame;

I humbly do beseech you of your pardon
For too much loving you.

OTHELLO.

I am bound to thee for ever.

IAGO.

I see this hath a little dash'd your spirits.

OTHELLO.

Not a jot, not a jot.

IAGO.

Trust me, I fear it has.
I hope you will consider what is spoke
Comes from my love; but I do see you're mov'd:—
I am to pray you not to strain my speech
To grosser issues nor to larger reach
Than to suspicion.

OTHELLO.

I will not.

IAGO.

Should you do so, my lord,
My speech should fall into such vile success
Which my thoughts aim'd not. Cassio's my worthy friend:—
My lord, I see you're mov'd.

OTHELLO.

No, not much mov'd.
I do not think but Desdemona's honest.

IAGO.

Long live she so! and long live you to think so!

OTHELLO.

And yet, how nature erring from itself,—

IAGO.

Ay, there's the point:—as,—to be bold with you,—
Not to affect many proposed matches,
Of her own clime, complexion, and degree,
Whereto we see in all things nature tends,—
Foh! one may smell in such a will most rank,
Foul disproportion, thoughts unnatural:—
But pardon me: I do not in position
Distinctly speak of her; though I may fear,

Her will, recoiling to her better judgement,
May fall to match you with her country forms,
And happily repent.

OTHELLO.

Farewell, farewell:
If more thou dost perceive, let me know more;
Set on thy wife to observe: leave me, Iago.

IAGO.

[Going.] My lord, I take my leave.

OTHELLO.

Why did I marry?—This honest creature doubtless
Sees and knows more, much more, than he unfolds.

IAGO.

[Returning.] My lord, I would I might entreat your honor
To scan this thing no further; leave it to time:
Though it be fit that Cassio have his place,—
For sure he fills it up with great ability,—
Yet, if you please to hold him off awhile,
You shall by that perceive him and his means:
Note if your lady strain his entertainment
With any strong or vehement importunity;
Much will be seen in that. In the meantime,
Let me be thought too busy in my fears,—
As worthy cause I have to fear I am,—
And hold her free, I do beseech your honor.

OTHELLO.

Fear not my government.

IAGO.

I once more take my leave.

[Exit.

OTHELLO.

This fellow's of exceeding honesty,
And knows all qualities, with a learned spirit,
Of human dealings. If I do prove her haggard,
Though that her jesses were my dear heartstrings,
I'd whistle her off, and let her down the wind
To prey at fortune. Haply, for I am black,
And have not those soft parts of conversation
That chamberers have; or for I am declin'd

Into the vale of years,—yet that's not much,—
She's gone; I am abus'd, and my relief
Must be to loathe her. O curse of marriage,
That we can call these delicate creatures ours,
And not their appetites! I had rather be a toad,
And live upon the vapor of a dungeon,
Than keep a corner in the thing I love
For others' uses. Yet, 'tis the plague of great ones:
Prerogativ'd are they less than the base;
'Tis destiny unshunnable, like death:
Even then this forked plague is fated to us
When we do quicken. Desdemona comes:
If she be false, O, then heaven mocks itself!—
I'll not believe't.

Re-enter DESDEMONA *and* EMILIA.

DESDEMONA.

How now, my dear Othello!
Your dinner, and the generous islanders
By you invited, do attend your presence.

OTHELLO.

I am to blame.

DESDEMONA.

Why do you speak so faintly?
Are you not well?

OTHELLO.

I have a pain upon my forehead here.

DESDEMONA.

Faith, that's with watching; 'twill away again;
Let me but bind it hard, within this hour
It will be well.

OTHELLO.

Your napkin is too little;
[He puts the handkerchief from him, and she drops it.]
Let it alone. Come, I'll go in with you.

DESDEMONA.

I am very sorry that you are not well.

[Exeunt OTHELLO *and* DESDEMONA.

EMILIA.

I am glad I have found this napkin;
This was her first remembrance from the Moor.
My wayward husband hath a hundred times
Woo'd me to steal it; but she so loves the token,—
For he conjur'd her she should ever keep it,—
That she reserves it evermore about her
To kiss and talk to. I'll have the work ta'en out,
And give't Iago:
What he will do with it heaven knows, not I;
I nothing but to please his fantasy.

Re-enter IAGO.

IAGO.

How now! what do you here alone?

EMILIA.

Do not you chide; I have a thing for you.

IAGO.

A thing for me!—it is a common thing.

EMILIA.

Ha!

IAGO.

To have a foolish wife.

EMILIA.

O, is that all? What will you give me now
For that same handkerchief?

IAGO.

What handkerchief?

EMILIA.

What handkerchief!
Why, that the Moor first gave to Desdemona;
That which so often you did bid me steal.

IAGO.

Hast stol'n it from her?

EMILIA.

No, faith; she let it drop by negligence,
And, to the advantage, I being here, took't up.
Look, here it is.

Emilia. What will you give me now
For that same handkerchief?
Iago. What handkerchief? *Act III. Scene III.*

IAGO.

A good wench; give it me.

EMILIA.

What will you do with't, that you have been so earnest
To have me filch it?

IAGO.

[Snatching it.] Why, what's that to you?

EMILIA.

If it be not for some purpose of import,
Give't me again: poor lady, she'll run mad
When she shall lack it.

IAGO.

Be not acknown on't; I have use for it.
Go, leave me.

[Exit EMILIA.

I will in Cassio's lodging lose this napkin,
And let him find it. Trifles light as air

Are to the jealous confirmations strong
As proofs of holy writ: this may do something.
The Moor already changes with my poison:
Dangerous conceits are in their natures poisons,
Which at the first are scarce found to distaste,
But, with a little act upon the blood,
Burn like the mines of sulphur.—I did say so:—
Look, where he comes!
Not poppy, nor mandragora,
Nor all the drowsy syrups of the world,
Shall ever medicine thee to that sweet sleep
Which thou ow'dst yesterday.

Re-enter OTHELLO.

OTHELLO.

Ha! ha! false to me?

IAGO.

Why, how now, general! no more of that.

OTHELLO.

Avaunt! be gone! thou hast set me on the rack:—
I swear 'tis better to be much abus'd
Than but to know't a little.

IAGO.

How now, my lord!

OTHELLO.

What sense had I of her stol'n hours of lust?
I saw't not, thought it not, it harm'd not me:
I slept the next night well, was free and merry;
I found not Cassio's kisses on her lips:
He that is robb'd, not wanting what is stol'n,
Let him not know't and he's not robb'd at all.

IAGO.

I am sorry to hear this.

OTHELLO.

I had been happy if the general camp,
Pioners and all, had tasted her sweet body,
So I had nothing known. O, now, for ever
Farewell the tranquil mind! farewell content!
Farewell the plumed troop and the big wars
That make ambition virtue! O, farewell,

Farewell the neighing steed and the shrill trump,
The spirit-stirring drum, the ear-piercing fife,
The royal banner, and all quality,
Pride, pomp, and circumstance of glorious war!
And, O you mortal engines, whose rude throats
The immortal Jove's dread clamors counterfeit,
Farewell! Othello's occupation's gone!

IAGO.

Is't possible, my lord?—

OTHELLO.

Villain, be sure thou prove my love a whore;—
[Taking him by the throat.]
Be sure of it. Give me the ocular proof;
Or, by the worth of man's eternal soul,
Thou hadst been better have been born a dog
Than answer my wak'd wrath!

IAGO.

Is't come to this?

OTHELLO.

Make me to see't; or at the least so prove it,
That the probation bear no hinge nor loop
To hang a doubt on; or woe upon thy life!

IAGO.

My noble lord,—

OTHELLO.

If thou dost slander her and torture me,
Never pray more; abandon all remorse;
On horror's head horrors accumulate;
Do deeds to make heaven weep, all earth amaz'd;
For nothing canst thou to damnation add
Greater than that.

IAGO.

O grace! O heaven defend me!
Are you a man? have you a soul or sense?—
God be wi' you; take mine office.—O wretched fool,
That liv'st to make thine honesty a vice!—
O monstrous world! Take note, take note, O world,
To be direct and honest is not safe.—
I thank you for this profit; and from hence
I'll love no friend, sith love breeds such offense.

OTHELLO.

Nay, stay:—thou shouldst be honest.

IAGO.

I should be wise; for honesty's a fool,
And loses that it works for.

OTHELLO.

By the world,
I think my wife be honest, and think she is not;
I think that thou art just, and think thou art not:
I'll have some proof: her name, that was as fresh
As Dian's visage, is now begrim'd and black
As mine own face.—If there be cords or knives,
Poison or fire, or suffocating streams,
I'll not endure 't.—Would I were satisfied!

IAGO.

I see, sir, you are eaten up with passion:
I do repent me that I put it to you.
You would be satisfied?

OTHELLO.

Would! nay, I will.

IAGO.

And may: but how? how satisfied, my lord?
Would you, the supervisor, grossly gape on,—
Behold her topp'd?

OTHELLO.

Death and damnation! O!

IAGO.

It were a tedious difficulty, I think,
To bring them to that prospect: damn them then,
If ever mortal eyes do see them bolster
More than their own! What then? how then?
What shall I say? Where's satisfaction?
It is impossible you should see this
Were they as prime as goats, as hot as monkeys,
As salt as wolves in pride, and fools as gross
As ignorance made drunk. But yet, I say,
If imputation and strong circumstances,—
Which lead directly to the door of truth,—
Will give you satisfaction, you may have't.

OTHELLO.

Give me a living reason she's disloyal.

IAGO.

I do not like the office;
But, sith I am enter'd in this cause so far,—
Prick'd to it by foolish honesty and love,—
I will go on. I lay with Cassio lately;
And, being troubled with a raging tooth,
I could not sleep.
There are a kind of men so loose of soul,
That in their sleeps will mutter their affairs:
One of this kind is Cassio:
In sleep I heard him say, "Sweet Desdemona,
Let us be wary, let us hide our loves";
And then, sir, would he gripe and wring my hand,
Cry, "O sweet creature!" and then kiss me hard,
As if he pluck'd up kisses by the roots,
That grew upon my lips: then laid his leg
Over my thigh, and sigh'd and kiss'd; and then
Cried, "Cursed fate that gave thee to the Moor!"

OTHELLO.

O monstrous! monstrous!

IAGO.

Nay, this was but his dream.

OTHELLO.

But this denoted a foregone conclusion:
'Tis a shrewd doubt, though it be but a dream.

IAGO.

And this may help to thicken other proofs
That do demonstrate thinly.

OTHELLO.

I'll tear her all to pieces.

IAGO.

Nay, but be wise: yet we see nothing done;
She may be honest yet. Tell me but this,—
Have you not sometimes seen a handkerchief
Spotted with strawberries in your wife's hand?

OTHELLO.

I gave her such a one; 'twas my first gift.

IAGO.

I know not that: but such a handkerchief,—
I am sure it was your wife's,—did I today
See Cassio wipe his beard with.

OTHELLO.

If it be that,—

IAGO.

If it be that, or any that was hers,
It speaks against her with the other proofs.

OTHELLO.

O, that the slave had forty thousand lives,—
One is too poor, too weak for my revenge!
Now do I see 'tis true.—Look here, Iago;
All my fond love thus do I blow to heaven:
'Tis gone.—
Arise, black vengeance, from thy hollow hell!
Yield up, O love, thy crown and hearted throne
To tyrannous hate! swell, bosom, with thy fraught,
For 'tis of aspics' tongues!

IAGO.

Yet be content.

OTHELLO.

O, blood, Iago, blood!

IAGO.

Patience, I say; your mind perhaps may change.

OTHELLO.

Never, Iago. Like to the Pontic Sea,
Whose icy current and compulsive course
Ne'er feels retiring ebb, but keeps due on
To the Propontic and the Hellespont;
Even so my bloody thoughts, with violent pace,
Shall ne'er look back, ne'er ebb to humble love,
Till that a capable and wide revenge
Swallow them up.—Now, by yond marble heaven,
In the due reverence of a sacred vow *[Kneels.]*
I here engage my words.

IAGO.

Do not rise yet.—*[Kneels.]*
Witness, you ever-burning lights above,
You elements that clip us round about,—
Witness that here Iago doth give up
The execution of his wit, hands, heart,
To wrong'd Othello's service! Let him command,
And to obey shall be in me remorse,
What bloody business ever. *[They rise.]*

OTHELLO.

I greet thy love,
Not with vain thanks, but with acceptance bounteous,
And will upon the instant put thee to't:
Within these three days let me hear thee say
That Cassio's not alive.

IAGO.

My friend is dead; 'tis done at your request:
But let her live.

OTHELLO.

Damn her, lewd minx! O, damn her!
Come, go with me apart; I will withdraw
To furnish me with some swift means of death
For the fair devil. Now art thou my lieutenant.

IAGO.

I am your own for ever.

[Exeunt.

SCENE IV. *Cyprus. Before the Castle.*

Enter DESDEMONA, EMILIA, *and* CLOWN.

DESDEMONA.
Do you know, sirrah, where Lieutenant Cassio lies?

CLOWN.
I dare not say he lies anywhere.

DESDEMONA.
Why, man?

CLOWN.
He's a soldier; and for one to say a soldier lies is stabbing.

DESDEMONA.

Go to: where lodges he?

CLOWN.

To tell you where he lodges is to tell you where I lie.

DESDEMONA.

Can anything be made of this?

CLOWN.

I know not where he lodges; and for me to devise a lodging, and say he lies here or he lies there were to lie in mine own throat.

DESDEMONA.

Can you inquire him out, and be edified by report?

CLOWN.

I will catechize the world for him; that is, make questions and by them answer.

DESDEMONA.

Seek him, bid him come hither: tell him I have moved my lord on his behalf, and hope all will be well.

CLOWN.

To do this is within the compass of man's wit; and therefore I will attempt the doing it.

[Exit.

DESDEMONA.

Where should I lose that handkerchief, Emilia?

EMILIA.

I know not, madam.

DESDEMONA.

Believe me, I had rather have lost my purse
Full of crusadoes: and, but my noble Moor
Is true of mind and made of no such baseness
As jealous creatures are, it were enough
To put him to ill thinking.

EMILIA.

Is he not jealous?

DESDEMONA.

Who, he? I think the sun where he was born
Drew all such humours from him.

Othello. Give me your hand: this hand is moist, my lady.
Desdemona. It yet has felt no age nor known no sorrow.
                                    Act III.   Scene IV.

EMILIA.

Look, where he comes.

DESDEMONA.

I will not leave him now till Cassio
Be call'd to him.

Enter OTHELLO.

How is't with you, my lord?

OTHELLO.

Well, my good lady.—*[Aside.]* O, hardness to dissemble!—
How do you, Desdemona?

DESDEMONA.

Well, my good lord.

OTHELLO.

Give me your hand: this hand is moist, my lady.

DESDEMONA.

It yet hath felt no age nor known no sorrow.

OTHELLO.

This argues fruitfulness and liberal heart:—
Hot, hot, and moist: this hand of yours requires
A sequester from liberty, fasting, and prayer,
Much castigation, exercise devout;
For here's a young and sweating devil here
That commonly rebels. 'Tis a good hand,
A frank one.

DESDEMONA.

You may, indeed, say so;
For 'twas that hand that gave away my heart.

OTHELLO.

A liberal hand: the hearts of old gave hands;
But our new heraldry is hands, not hearts.

DESDEMONA.

I cannot speak of this. Come now, your promise.

OTHELLO.

What promise, chuck?

DESDEMONA.

I have sent to bid Cassio come speak with you.

OTHELLO.

I have a salt and sorry rheum offends me;
Lend me thy handkerchief.

DESDEMONA.

Here, my lord.

OTHELLO.

That which I gave you.

DESDEMONA.

I have it not about me.

OTHELLO.

Not?

DESDEMONA.

No, faith, my lord.

OTHELLO.

That is a fault. That handkerchief
Did an Egyptian to my mother give;
She was a charmer, and could almost read
The thoughts of people: she told her, while she kept it,
'Twould make her amiable and subdue my father
Entirely to her love; but if she lost it
Or made a gift of it, my father's eye
Should hold her loathed, and his spirits should hunt
After new fancies: she, dying, gave it me;
And bid me, when my fate would have me wive,
To give it her. I did so: and take heed on't;
Make it a darling like your precious eye;
To lose't or give't away were such perdition
As nothing else could match.

DESDEMONA.

Is't possible?

OTHELLO.

'Tis true: there's magic in the web of it:
A sibyl, that had number'd in the world
The sun to course two hundred compasses,
In her prophetic fury sew'd the work;
The worms were hallow'd that did breed the silk;
And it was dy'd in mummy which the skillful
Conserv'd of maiden's hearts.

DESDEMONA.

Indeed! is't true?

OTHELLO.

Most veritable; therefore look to't well.

DESDEMONA.

Then would to God that I had never seen't!

OTHELLO.

Ha! wherefore?

DESDEMONA.

Why do you speak so startingly and rash?

OTHELLO.

Is't lost? is't gone? speak, is it out of the way?

DESDEMONA.

Heaven bless us!

OTHELLO.

Say you?

DESDEMONA.

It is not lost; but what an if it were?

OTHELLO.

How!

DESDEMONA.

I say, it is not lost.

OTHELLO.

Fetch't, let me see't.

DESDEMONA.

Why, so I can, sir, but I will not now.
This is a trick to put me from my suit:
Pray you, let Cassio be receiv'd again.

OTHELLO.

Fetch me the handkerchief: my mind misgives.

DESDEMONA.

Come, come;
You'll never meet a more sufficient man.

OTHELLO.

The handkerchief!

DESDEMONA.

I pray, talk me of Cassio.

OTHELLO.

The handkerchief!

DESDEMONA.

A man that all his time
Hath founded his good fortunes on your love,
Shar'd dangers with you,—

OTHELLO.

The handkerchief!

DESDEMONA.

In sooth, you are to blame.

OTHELLO.

Away!

                                                        [Exit.

EMILIA.

Is not this man jealous?

DESDEMONA.

I ne'er saw this before.
Sure there's some wonder in this handkerchief;
I am most unhappy in the loss of it.

EMILIA.

'Tis not a year or two shows us a man:
They are all but stomachs and we all but food:
They eat us hungerly, and when they are full,
They belch us.—Look you,—Cassio and my husband.

Enter CASSIO *and* IAGO.

IAGO.

There is no other way; 'tis she must do't:
And, lo, the happiness! go and importune her.

DESDEMONA.

How now, good Cassio! what's the news with you?

CASSIO.

Madam, my former suit: I do beseech you
That by your virtuous means I may again
Exist, and be a member of his love,
Whom I, with all the office of my heart,
Entirely honor: I would not be delay'd.
If my offence be of such mortal kind
That nor my service past, nor present sorrows,
Nor purpos'd merit in futurity,
Can ransom me into his love again,
But to know so must be my benefit;
So shall I clothe me in a forc'd content,
And shut myself up in some other course,
To fortune's alms.

DESDEMONA.

Alas, thrice-gentle Cassio!
My advocation is not now in tune;
My lord is not my lord; nor should I know him
Were he in favor as in humour alter'd.
So help me every spirit sanctified,
As I have spoken for you all my best,
And stood within the blank of his displeasure
For my free speech! You must awhile be patient:
What I can do I will; and more I will
Than for myself I dare: let that suffice you.

IAGO.

Is my lord angry?

EMILIA.

He went hence but now,
And certainly in strange unquietness.

IAGO.

Can he be angry? I have seen the cannon,
When it hath blown his ranks into the air
And, like the devil, from his very arm
Puff'd his own brother;—and can he be angry?
Something of moment, then: I will go meet him:
There's matter in't indeed if he be angry.

DESDEMONA.

I pr'ythee, do so.

[Exit IAGO.

Something sure of state,—
Either from Venice or some unhatch'd practice
Made demonstrable here in Cyprus to him,—
Hath puddled his clear spirit, and in such cases
Men's natures wrangle with inferior things,
Though great ones are their object. 'Tis even so;
For let our finger ache, and it indues
Our other healthful members even to that sense
Of pain: nay, we must think men are not gods,
Nor of them look for such observancy
As fits the bridal.—Beshrew me much, Emilia,
I was,—unhandsome warrior as I am,—
Arraigning his unkindness with my soul;

But now I find I had suborn'd the witness,
And he's indicted falsely.

EMILIA.

Pray heaven it be state matters, as you think,
And no conception nor no jealous toy
Concerning you.

DESDEMONA.

Alas the day, I never gave him cause!

EMILIA.

But jealous souls will not be answer'd so;
They are not ever jealous for the cause,
But jealous for they are jealous: 'tis a monster
Begot upon itself, born on itself.

DESDEMONA.

Heaven keep that monster from Othello's mind!

EMILIA.

Lady, amen.

DESDEMONA.

I will go seek him.—Cassio, walk hereabout:
If I do find him fit, I'll move your suit,
And seek to effect it to my uttermost.

CASSIO.

I humbly thank your ladyship.

[*Exeunt* DESDEMONA *and* EMILIA.

Enter BIANCA.

BIANCA.

Save you, friend Cassio!

CASSIO.

What make you from home?
How is it with you, my most fair Bianca?
I'faith, sweet love, I was coming to your house.

BIANCA.

And I was going to your lodging, Cassio.
What, keep a week away? seven days and nights?
Eight score eight hours? and lovers' absent hours,
More tedious than the dial eight score times?
O weary reckoning!

CASSIO.

Pardon me, Bianca:
I have this while with leaden thoughts been press'd;
But I shall in a more continuate time
Strike off this score of absence. Sweet Bianca,
[Giving her DESDEMONA's *handkerchief.]*
Take me this work out.

Cassio.   Sweet Bianca,
Take me this work out.
    Bianca.   O Cassio! whence came this?   Act III.   Scene IV.

BIANCA.

O Cassio, whence came this?
This is some token from a newer friend.
To the felt absence now I feel a cause:
Is't come to this? Well, well.

CASSIO.

Go to, woman!
Throw your vile guesses in the devil's teeth,
From whence you have them. You are jealous now
That this is from some mistress, some remembrance:
No, in good troth, Bianca.

BIANCA.

Why, whose is it?

CASSIO.

I know not, sweet: I found it in my chamber.
I like the work well: ere it be demanded,—
As like enough it will,—I'd have it copied:
Take it, and do't; and leave me for this time.

BIANCA.

Leave you! wherefore?

CASSIO.

I do attend here on the general;
And think it no addition, nor my wish,
To have him see me woman'd.

BIANCA.

Why, I pray you?

CASSIO.

Not that I love you not.

BIANCA.

But that you do not love me.
I pray you, bring me on the way a little;
And say if I shall see you soon at night.

CASSIO.

'Tis but a little way that I can bring you,
For I attend here: but I'll see you soon.

BIANCA.

'Tis very good; I must be circumstanc'd.

[Exeunt.

ACT IV.

SCENE I. *Cyprus. Before the Castle.*

Enter OTHELLO *and* IAGO.

IAGO.

Will you think so?

OTHELLO.

Think so, Iago?

IAGO.

What,
To kiss in private?

OTHELLO.

An unauthoriz'd kiss.

IAGO.

Or to be naked with her friend in bed
An hour or more, not meaning any harm?

OTHELLO.

Naked in bed, Iago, and not mean harm!
It is hypocrisy against the devil:
They that mean virtuously and yet do so,
The devil their virtue tempts, and they tempt heaven.

IAGO.

So they do nothing, 'tis a venial slip:
But if I give my wife a handkerchief,—

OTHELLO.

What then?

IAGO.

Why, then, 'tis hers, my lord, and being hers,
She may, I think, bestow't on any man.

OTHELLO.

She is protectress of her honor too:
May she give that?

IAGO.

Her honor is an essence that's not seen;
They have it very oft that have it not:
But, for the handkerchief,—

OTHELLO.

By heaven, I would most gladly have forgot it:—
Thou said'st,—O, it comes o'er my memory,
As doth the raven o'er the infected house,
Boding to all,—he had my handkerchief.

IAGO.

Ay, what of that?

OTHELLO.

That's not so good now.

IAGO.

What,
If I had said I had seen him do you wrong?
Or heard him say,—as knaves be such abroad,
Who having, by their own importunate suit,
Or voluntary dotage of some mistress,
Convinced or supplied them, cannot choose
But they must blab,—

OTHELLO.

Hath he said anything?

IAGO.

He hath, my lord; but be you well assur'd,
No more than he'll unswear.

OTHELLO.

What hath he said?

IAGO.

Faith, that he did,—I know not what he did.

OTHELLO.

What? what?

IAGO.

Lie,—

OTHELLO.

With her?

IAGO.

With her, on her, what you will.

OTHELLO.

That's fulsome.—Handkerchief—confessions— handkerchief!—
To confess, and be hanged for his labour,—first, to be hanged, and
then to confess.—I tremble at it. Nature would not invest herself in such shadowing passion without some instruction. It is
not words that shake me thus:—pish!—Is't possible?—Confess,—
handkerchief!—O devil!—

[Falls in a trance.]

Iago. Work on,
My medicine, work! Thus credulous fools are caught.
Act IV. Scene I.

IAGO.

Work on,
My medicine, work! Thus credulous fools are caught;
And many worthy and chaste dames even thus,
All guiltless, meet reproach.—What, ho! my lord!
My lord, I say! Othello!

Enter CASSIO.

How now, Cassio!

CASSIO.

What's the matter?

IAGO.

My lord is fallen into an epilepsy:
This is his second fit; he had one yesterday.

CASSIO.

Rub him about the temples.

IAGO.

No, forbear;
The lethargy must have his quiet course:
If not, he foams at mouth, and by and by
Breaks out to savage madness. Look, he stirs:
Do you withdraw yourself a little while,
He will recover straight: when he is gone,
I would on great occasion speak with you.

[Exit CASSIO.

How is it, general? have you not hurt your head?

OTHELLO.

Dost thou mock me?

IAGO.

I mock you! no, by heaven.
Would you would bear your fortune like a man!

OTHELLO.

A horned man's a monster and a beast.

IAGO.

There's many a beast, then, in a populous city,
And many a civil monster.

OTHELLO.

Did he confess it?

IAGO.

Good sir, be a man;
Think every bearded fellow that's but yok'd
May draw with you: there's millions now alive
That nightly lie in those unproper beds
Which they dare swear peculiar: your case is better.
O, 'tis the spite of hell, the fiend's arch-mock,
To lip a wanton in a secure couch,
And to suppose her chaste! No, let me know;
And knowing what I am, I know what she shall be.

OTHELLO.

O, thou art wise; 'tis certain.

IAGO.

Stand you awhile apart;
Confine yourself but in a patient list.
Whilst you were here o'erwhelmed with your grief,—
A passion most unsuiting such a man,—
Cassio came hither: I shifted him away,
And laid good 'scuse upon your ecstasy;
Bade him anon return, and here speak with me;
The which he promis'd. Do but encave yourself,
And mark the fleers, the gibes, and notable scorns,
That dwell in every region of his face;
For I will make him tell the tale anew,—
Where, how, how oft, how long ago, and when
He hath, and is again to cope your wife:
I say, but mark his gesture. Marry, patience;
Or I shall say you are all in all in spleen,
And nothing of a man.

OTHELLO.

Dost thou hear, Iago?
I will be found most cunning in my patience;
But,—dost thou hear?—most bloody.

IAGO.

That's not amiss;
But yet keep time in all. Will you withdraw?

[OTHELLO withdraws.]

Now will I question Cassio of Bianca,
A housewife that, by selling her desires,

Buys herself bread and clothes: it is a creature
That dotes on Cassio,—as 'tis the strumpet's plague
To beguile many and be beguil'd by one:—
He, when he hears of her, cannot refrain
From the excess of laughter:—here he comes:—
As he shall smile Othello shall go mad;
And his unbookish jealousy must construe
Poor Cassio's smiles, gestures, and light behavior
Quite in the wrong.

Re-enter CASSIO.

How do you now, lieutenant?

CASSIO.

The worser that you give me the addition
Whose want even kills me.

IAGO.

Ply Desdemona well, and you are sure on't.
[Speaking lower.] Now, if this suit lay in Bianca's power,
How quickly should you speed!

CASSIO.

Alas, poor caitiff!

OTHELLO.

[Aside.] Look, how he laughs already!

IAGO.

I never knew a woman love man so.

CASSIO.

Alas, poor rogue! I think, i'faith, she loves me.

OTHELLO.

[Aside.] Now he denies it faintly and laughs it out.

IAGO.

Do you hear, Cassio?

OTHELLO.

[Aside.] Now he importunes him
To tell it o'er: go to; well said, well said.

IAGO.

She gives it out that you shall marry her:
Do you intend it?

CASSIO.

Ha, ha, ha!

OTHELLO.

[Aside.] Do you triumph, Roman? do you triumph?

CASSIO.

I marry her!—what? A customer! I pr'ythee, bear some charity to my wit; do not think it so unwholesome:—ha, ha, ha!

OTHELLO.

[Aside.] So, so, so, so: they laugh that win.

IAGO.

Faith, the cry goes that you shall marry her.

CASSIO.

Pr'ythee, say true.

IAGO.

I am a very villain else.

OTHELLO.

[Aside.] Have you scored me? Well.

CASSIO.

This is the monkey's own giving out: she is persuaded I will marry her, out of her own love and flattery, not out of my promise.

OTHELLO.

[Aside.] Iago beckons me; now he begins the story.

CASSIO.

She was here even now; she haunts me in every place. I was the other day talking on the sea bank with certain Venetians, and thither comes the bauble, and, by this hand, she falls me thus about my neck,—

OTHELLO.

[Aside.] Crying, "O dear Cassio!" as it were: his gesture imports it.

CASSIO.

So hangs, and lolls, and weeps upon me; so hales and pulls me: ha, ha, ha!

OTHELLO.

[Aside.] Now he tells how she plucked him to my chamber. O, I see that nose of yours, but not that dog I shall throw it to.

CASSIO.

Well, I must leave her company.

IAGO.

Before me! look where she comes.

CASSIO.

'Tis such another fitchew! marry, a perfumed one.

Enter BIANCA.

What do you mean by this haunting of me?

BIANCA.

Let the devil and his dam haunt you! What did you mean by that same handkerchief you gave me even now? I was a fine fool to take it. I must take out the work?—A likely piece of work that you should find it in your chamber and not know who left it there! This is some minx's token, and I must take out the work? There,—give it your hobby-horse: wheresoever you had it, I'll take out no work on't.

CASSIO.

How now, my sweet Bianca! how now! how now!

OTHELLO.

[Aside.] By heaven, that should be my handkerchief!

BIANCA.

An you'll come to supper to-night, you may; an you will not, come when you are next prepared for.

[Exit.

IAGO.

After her, after her.

CASSIO.

Faith, I must; she'll rail in the street else.

IAGO.

Will you sup there?

CASSIO.

Faith, I intend so.

IAGO.

Well, I may chance to see you; for I would very fain speak with you.

CASSIO.

Pr'ythee, come; will you?

IAGO.

Go to; say no more.

[Exit CASSIO.

OTHELLO.

[Coming forward.] How shall I murder him, Iago?

IAGO.

Did you perceive how he laughed at his vice?

OTHELLO.

O Iago!

IAGO.

And did you see the handkerchief?

OTHELLO.

Was that mine?

IAGO.

Yours, by this hand: and to see how he prizes the foolish woman your wife! she gave it him, and he hath given it his whore.

OTHELLO.

I would have him nine years a-killing.—A fine woman! a fair woman! a sweet woman!

IAGO.

Nay, you must forget that.

OTHELLO.

Ay, let her rot, and perish, and be damned to-night; for she shall not live: no, my heart is turned to stone; I strike it, and it hurts my hand.—O, the world hath not a sweeter creature: she might lie by an emperor's side, and command him tasks.

IAGO.

Nay, that's not your way.

OTHELLO.

Hang her! I do but say what she is:—so delicate with her needle!—an admirable musician! O, she will sing the savageness out of a bear!—Of so high and plenteous wit and invention!—

IAGO.

She's the worse for all this.

OTHELLO.

O, a thousand, a thousand times:—and then, of so gentle a condition!

IAGO.

Ay, too gentle.

OTHELLO.

Nay, that's certain:—but yet the pity of it, Iago!
O Iago, the pity of it, Iago!

IAGO.

If you are so fond over her iniquity, give her patent to offend; for,
if it touch not you, it comes near nobody.

OTHELLO.

I will chop her into messes.—Cuckold me!

IAGO.

O, 'tis foul in her.

OTHELLO.

With mine officer!

IAGO.

That's fouler.

OTHELLO.

Get me some poison, Iago; this night.—I'll not expostulate with
her, lest her body and beauty unprovide my mind again:— this
night, Iago.

IAGO.

Do it not with poison; strangle her in her bed, even the bed she
hath contaminated.

OTHELLO.

Good, good: the justice of it pleases: very good.

IAGO.

And for Cassio,—let me be his undertaker:—you shall hear more
by midnight.

OTHELLO.

Excellent good. *[A trumpet within.]* What trumpet is that same?

IAGO.

Something from Venice, sure. 'Tis Lodovico
Come from the duke: and, see, your wife is with him.

Enter LODOVICO, DESDEMONA, *and Attendants.*

LODOVICO.

Save you, worthy general!

OTHELLO.

With all my heart, sir.

LODOVICO.

The duke and senators of Venice greet you.
[Gives him a packet.]

OTHELLO.

I kiss the instrument of their pleasures.
[Opens the packet and reads.]

DESDEMONA.

And what's the news, good cousin Lodovico?

IAGO.

I am very glad to see you, signior;
Welcome to Cyprus.

LODOVICO.

I thank you. How does Lieutenant Cassio?

IAGO.

Lives, sir.

DESDEMONA.

Cousin, there's fall'n between him and my lord
An unkind breach: but you shall make all well.

OTHELLO.

Are you sure of that?

DESDEMONA.

My lord?

OTHELLO.

[Reads.] "This fail you not to do, as you will,—"

LODOVICO.

He did not call; he's busy in the paper.
Is there division 'twixt my lord and Cassio?

DESDEMONA.

A most unhappy one: I would do much
To atone them, for the love I bear to Cassio.

OTHELLO.

Fire and brimstone!

DESDEMONA.

My lord?

OTHELLO.

Are you wise?

DESDEMONA.

What, is he angry?

LODOVICO.

May be the letter mov'd him;
For, as I think, they do command him home,
Deputing Cassio in his government.

DESDEMONA.

Trust me, I am glad on't.

OTHELLO.

Indeed!

DESDEMONA.

My lord?

OTHELLO.

I am glad to see you mad.

DESDEMONA.

Why, sweet Othello,—

OTHELLO.

Devil! *[Striking her.]*

DESDEMONA.

I have not deserv'd this.

LODOVICO.

My lord, this would not be believ'd in Venice,
Though I should swear I saw't: 'tis very much:
Make her amends; she weeps.

OTHELLO.

O devil, devil!
If that the earth could teem with woman's tears,
Each drop she falls would prove a crocodile.—
Out of my sight!

DESDEMONA.

[Going.] I will not stay to offend you.

LODOVICO.

Truly, an obedient lady:—
I do beseech your lordship, call her back.

OTHELLO.

Mistress!

DESDEMONA.

My lord?

OTHELLO.

What would you with her, sir?

LODOVICO.

Who, I, my lord?

OTHELLO.

Ay; you did wish that I would make her turn:
Sir, she can turn, and turn, and yet go on,
And turn again; and she can weep, sir, weep;
And she's obedient, as you say,—obedient,—
Very obedient.—Proceed you in your tears.—
Concerning this, sir,—O well-painted passion!
I am commanded home.—Get you away;
I'll send for you anon.—Sir, I obey the mandate,
And will return to Venice.—Hence, avaunt!

[Exit DESDEMONA.

Cassio shall have my place. And, sir, to-night,
I do entreat that we may sup together:
You are welcome, sir, to Cyprus.—Goats and monkeys!

[Exit.

LODOVICO.

Is this the noble Moor whom our full senate
Call all-in-all sufficient? this the noble nature
Whom passion could not shake? whose solid virtue
The shot of accident nor dart of chance
Could neither graze nor pierce?

IAGO.

He is much chang'd.

LODOVICO.

Are his wits safe? is he not light of brain?

IAGO.

He's that he is: I may not breathe my censure
What he might be,—if what he might he is not,—
I would to heaven he were!

LODOVICO.

What, strike his wife!

IAGO.

Faith, that was not so well; yet would I knew
That stroke would prove the worst!

LODOVICO.

Is it his use?
Or did the letters work upon his blood,
And new-create this fault?

IAGO.

Alas, alas!
It is not honesty in me to speak
What I have seen and known. You shall observe him;
And his own courses will denote him so
That I may save my speech: do but go after,
And mark how he continues.

LODOVICO.

I am sorry that I am deceiv'd in him.

[Exeunt.

SCENE II. *Cyprus. A Room in the Castle.*

Enter OTHELLO *and* EMILIA.

OTHELLO.

You have seen nothing, then?

EMILIA.

Nor ever heard, nor ever did suspect.

OTHELLO.

Yes, you have seen Cassio and she together.

EMILIA.

But then I saw no harm, and then I heard
Each syllable that breath made up between them.

OTHELLO.

What, did they never whisper?

EMILIA.

Never, my lord.

OTHELLO.

Nor send you out o' the way?

EMILIA.

Never.

OTHELLO.

To fetch her fan, her gloves, her mask, nor nothing?

EMILIA.

Never, my lord.

OTHELLO.

That's strange.

EMILIA.

I durst, my lord, to wager she is honest,
Lay down my soul at stake: if you think other,
Remove your thought,—it doth abuse your bosom.
If any wretch have put this in your head,
Let heaven requite it with the serpent's curse!
For if she be not honest, chaste, and true,
There's no man happy; the purest of their wives
Is foul as slander.

OTHELLO.

Bid her come hither.—Go.

[Exit EMILIA.

She says enough; yet she's a simple bawd
That cannot say as much. This is a subtle whore,
A closet-lock-and-key of villainous secrets:
And yet she'll kneel and pray; I have seen her do't.

Enter EMILIA *with* DESDEMONA.

DESDEMONA.

My lord, what is your will?

OTHELLO.

Pray, chuck, come hither.

DESDEMONA.

What is your pleasure?

OTHELLO.

Let me see your eyes;
Look in my face.

DESDEMONA.

What horrible fancy's this?

OTHELLO.

Some of your function, mistress, *[To* EMILIA.*]*
Leave procreants alone and shut the door;
Cough, or cry hem, if anybody come.
Your mystery, your mystery;—nay, despatch.

[Exit EMILIA.

DESDEMONA.

Upon my knees, what doth your speech import?
I understand a fury in your words,
But not the words.

OTHELLO.

Why, what art thou?

DESDEMONA.

Your wife, my lord; your true and loyal wife.

OTHELLO.

Come, swear it, damn thyself;
Lest, being like one of heaven, the devils themselves
Should fear to seize thee: therefore be double-damn'd.—
Swear thou art honest.

DESDEMONA.

Heaven doth truly know it.

OTHELLO.

Heaven truly knows that thou art false as hell.

DESDEMONA.

To whom, my lord? with whom? how am I false?

OTHELLO.

O Desdemona!—away! away! away!

DESDEMONA.

Alas the heavy day!—Why do you weep?
Am I the motive of these tears, my lord?
If haply you my father do suspect
An instrument of this your calling back,
Lay not your blame on me: if you have lost him,
Why, I have lost him too.

OTHELLO.

Had it pleas'd heaven
To try me with affliction; had they rain'd

All kinds of sores and shames on my bare head;
Steep'd me in poverty to the very lips;
Given to captivity me and my utmost hopes;
I should have found in some place of my soul
A drop of patience: but, alas, to make me
A fixed figure for the time, for scorn
To point his slow unmoving finger at!—
Yet could I bear that too; well, very well:
But there, where I have garner'd up my heart;
Where either I must live or bear no life,—
The fountain from the which my current runs,
Or else dries up; to be discarded thence!
Or keep it as a cistern for foul toads
To knot and gender in!—turn thy complexion there,
Patience, thou young and rose-lipp'd cherubin,—
Ay, there, look grim as hell!

DESDEMONA.

I hope my noble lord esteems me honest.

OTHELLO.

O, ay; as summer flies are in the shambles,
That quicken even with blowing. O thou weed,
Who art so lovely fair, and smell'st so sweet,
That the sense aches at thee,—would thou hadst ne'er been born!

DESDEMONA.

Alas, what ignorant sin have I committed?

OTHELLO.

Was this fair paper, this most goodly book,
Made to write "whore" upon? What committed!
Committed!—O thou public commoner!
I should make very forges of my cheeks,
That would to cinders burn up modesty,
Did I but speak thy deeds.—What committed!
Heaven stops the nose at it, and the moon winks;
The bawdy wind, that kisses all it meets,
Is hush'd within the hollow mine of earth,
And will not hear it.—What committed!—
Impudent strumpet!

DESDEMONA.

By heaven, you do me wrong.

OTHELLO.

Are not you a strumpet?

DESDEMONA.

No, as I am a Christian:
If to preserve this vessel for my lord
From any other foul unlawful touch
Be not to be a strumpet, I am none.

OTHELLO.

What, not a whore?

DESDEMONA.

No, as I shall be sav'd.

OTHELLO.

Is't possible?

DESDEMONA.

O, heaven forgive us!

OTHELLO.

I cry you mercy then:
I took you for that cunning whore of Venice
That married with Othello.—You, mistress,
That have the office opposite to Saint Peter,
And keep the gate of hell!

Re-enter EMILIA.

You, you, ay, you!
We have done our course; there's money for your pains:
I pray you, turn the key, and keep our counsel.

[Exit.

EMILIA.

Alas, what does this gentleman conceive?—
How do you, madam? how do you, my good lady?

DESDEMONA.

Faith, half asleep.

EMILIA.

Good madam, what's the matter with my lord?

DESDEMONA.

With who?

EMILIA.

Why, with my lord, madam.

Emilia.   How do you, madam? how do you, my good lady?
Desdemona.   Faith, half asleep.   *Act IV.   Scene II.*

DESDEMONA.

Who is thy lord?

EMILIA.

He that is yours, sweet lady.

DESDEMONA.

I have none: do not talk to me, Emilia;
I cannot weep; nor answer have I none
But what should go by water. Pr'ythee, to-night
Lay on my bed my wedding sheets,—remember;—
And call thy husband hither.

EMILIA.

Here's a change indeed!

[Exit.

DESDEMONA.

'Tis meet I should be us'd so, very meet.
How have I been behav'd, that he might stick
The small'st opinion on my least misuse?

Re-enter EMILIA *with* IAGO.

IAGO.

What is your pleasure, madam? How is't with you?

DESDEMONA.

I cannot tell. Those that do teach young babes
Do it with gentle means and easy tasks:
He might have chid me so; for in good faith,
I am a child to chiding.

IAGO.

What's the matter, lady?

EMILIA.

Alas, Iago, my lord hath so bewhor'd her,
Thrown such despite and heavy terms upon her,
As true hearts cannot bear.

DESDEMONA.

Am I that name, Iago?

IAGO.

What name, fair lady?

DESDEMONA.

Such as she says my lord did say I was.

EMILIA.

He call'd her whore: a beggar in his drink
Could not have laid such terms upon his callet.

IAGO.

Why did he so?

DESDEMONA.

I do not know; I am sure I am none such.

IAGO.

Do not weep, do not weep:—alas the day!

EMILIA.

Hath she forsook so many noble matches,
Her father, and her country, and her friends,
To be call'd whore? would it not make one weep?

DESDEMONA.

It is my wretched fortune.

IAGO.

Beshrew him for't!
How comes this trick upon him?

DESDEMONA.

Nay, heaven doth know.

EMILIA.

I will be hang'd, if some eternal villain,
Some busy and insinuating rogue,
Some cogging, cozening slave, to get some office,
Have not devis'd this slander; I'll be hang'd else.

IAGO.

Fie, there is no such man; it is impossible.

DESDEMONA.

If any such there be, heaven pardon him!

EMILIA.

A halter pardon him! and hell gnaw his bones!
Why should he call her whore? who keeps her company?
What place? what time? what form? what likelihood?
The Moor's abused by some most villainous knave,
Some base notorious knave, some scurvy fellow:—
O heaven, that such companions thou'dst unfold,
And put in every honest hand a whip
To lash the rascals naked through the world
Even from the east to the west!

IAGO.

Speak within door.

EMILIA.

O, fie upon them! some such squire he was
That turn'd your wit the seamy side without,
And made you to suspect me with the Moor.

IAGO.

You are a fool; go to.

DESDEMONA.

Oh, good Iago,
What shall I do to win my lord again?
Good friend, go to him; for by this light of heaven,
I know not how I lost him. Here I kneel:—
If e'er my will did trespass 'gainst his love,
Either in discourse of thought or actual deed;
Or that mine eyes, mine ears, or any sense,
Delighted them in any other form;

Or that I do not yet, and ever did,
And ever will, though he do shake me off
To beggarly divorcement,—love him dearly,
Comfort forswear me! Unkindness may do much;
And his unkindness may defeat my life,
But never taint my love. I cannot say "whore,"—
It does abhor me now I speak the word;
To do the act that might the addition earn
Not the world's mass of vanity could make me.

IAGO.

I pray you, be content; 'tis but his humour:
The business of the state does him offence,
And he does chide with you.

DESDEMONA.

If 'twere no other,—

IAGO.

'Tis but so, I warrant.
[Trumpets within.]
Hark, how these instruments summon to supper!
The messengers of Venice stay the meat:
Go in, and weep not; all things shall be well.

[Exeunt DESDEMONA *and* EMILIA.

Enter RODERIGO.

How now, Roderigo!

RODERIGO.

I do not find that thou dealest justly with me.

IAGO.

What in the contrary?

RODERIGO.

Every day thou daffest me with some device, Iago; and rather, as
it seems to me now, keepest from me all conveniency than suppli-
est me with the least advantage of hope. I will indeed no longer
endure it; nor am I yet persuaded to put up in peace what already
I have foolishly suffered.

IAGO.

Will you hear me, Roderigo?

Roderigo.

Faith, I have heard too much; for your words and performances are no kin together.

Iago.

You charge me most unjustly.

Roderigo.

With naught but truth. I have wasted myself out of my means. The jewels you have had from me to deliver to Desdemona would half have corrupted a votarist: you have told me she hath received them, and returned me expectations and comforts of sudden respect and acquaintance; but I find none.

Iago.

Well; go to; very well.

Roderigo.

Very well! go to! I cannot go to, man; nor 'tis not very well: by this hand, I say, 'tis very scurvy, and begin to find myself fobbed in it.

Iago.

Very well.

Roderigo.

I tell you 'tis not very well. I will make myself known to Desdemona: if she will return me my jewels, I will give over my suit and repent my unlawful solicitation; if not, assure yourself I will seek satisfaction of you.

Iago.

You have said now.

Roderigo.

Ay, and said nothing but what I protest intendment of doing.

Iago.

Why, now I see there's mettle in thee; and even from this instant do build on thee a better opinion than ever before. Give me thy hand, Roderigo. Thou hast taken against me a most just exception; but yet, I protest, I have dealt most directly in thy affair.

Roderigo.

It hath not appeared.

Iago.

I grant indeed it hath not appeared, and your suspicion is not without wit and judgement. But, Roderigo, if thou hast that in thee indeed, which I have greater reason to believe now than ever,—I mean purpose, courage, and valour,—this night show it: if thou the next night following enjoy not Desdemona, take me from this world with treachery and devise engines for my life.

RODERIGO.

Well, what is it? is it within reason and compass?

IAGO.

Sir, there is especial commission come from Venice to depute Cassio in Othello's place.

RODERIGO.

Is that true? why then Othello and Desdemona return again to Venice.

IAGO.

O, no; he goes into Mauritania, and takes away with him the fair Desdemona, unless his abode be lingered here by some accident: wherein none can be so determinate as the removing of Cassio.

RODERIGO.

How do you mean "removing" of him?

IAGO.

Why, by making him uncapable of Othello's place;—knocking out his brains.

RODERIGO.

And that you would have me to do?

IAGO.

Ay, if you dare do yourself a profit and a right. He sups to-night with a harlotry, and thither will I go to him:—he knows not yet of his honorable fortune. If you will watch his going thence,—which I will fashion to fall out between twelve and one,—you may take him at your pleasure: I will be near to second your attempt, and he shall fall between us. Come, stand not amazed at it, but go along with me; I will show you such a necessity in his death that you shall think yourself bound to put it on him. It is now high supper-time, and the night grows to waste: about it.

RODERIGO.

I will hear further reason for this.

IAGO.

And you shall be satisfied.

[*Exeunt.*

SCENE III. *Cyprus. Another Room in the Castle.*

Enter OTHELLO, LODOVICO, DESDEMONA, EMILIA, *and Attendants.*

LODOVICO.

I do beseech you, sir, trouble yourself no further.

OTHELLO.

O, pardon me; 'twill do me good to walk.

LODOVICO.

Madam, good night; I humbly thank your ladyship.

DESDEMONA.

Your honor is most welcome.

OTHELLO.

Will you walk, sir?—
O,—Desdemona,—

DESDEMONA.

My lord?

OTHELLO.

Get you to bed on the instant; I will be returned forthwith: dismiss
your attendant there: look't be done.

DESDEMONA.

I will, my lord.

[*Exeunt* OTHELLO, LODOVICO, *and Attendants.*

EMILIA.

How goes it now? he looks gentler than he did.

DESDEMONA.

He says he will return incontinent:
He hath commanded me to go to bed,
And bade me to dismiss you.

EMILIA.

Dismiss me!

DESDEMONA.

It was his bidding; therefore, good Emilia,
Give me my nightly wearing, and adieu:
We must not now displease him.

EMILIA.

I would you had never seen him!

DESDEMONA.

So would not I: my love doth so approve him,
That even his stubbornness, his checks, his frowns,—
Pr'ythee, unpin me,—have grace and favor in them.

EMILIA.

I have laid those sheets you bade me on the bed.

DESDEMONA.

All's one.—Good faith, how foolish are our minds!—
If I do die before thee, pr'ythee, shroud me
In one of those same sheets.

EMILIA.

Come, come, you talk.

DESDEMONA.

My mother had a maid call'd Barbara;
She was in love; and he she lov'd prov'd mad
And did forsake her: she had a song of "willow";
An old thing 'twas, but it express'd her fortune,
And she died singing it: that song to-night
Will not go from my mind; I have much to do
But to go hang my head all at one side,
And sing it like poor Barbara. Pr'ythee, despatch.

EMILIA.

Shall I go fetch your night-gown?

DESDEMONA.

No, unpin me here.—
This Lodovico is a proper man.

EMILIA.

A very handsome man.

DESDEMONA.

He speaks well.

EMILIA.

I know a lady in Venice would have walked barefoot to
Palestine for a touch of his nether lip.

DESDEMONA.

[Sings.]

> "The poor soul sat sighing by a sycamore tree,
>   Sing all a green willow;
> Her hand on her bosom, her head on her knee,
>   Sing willow, willow, willow:
> The fresh streams ran by her, and murmur'd her moans;
>   Sing willow, willow, willow;
> Her salt tears fell from her, and soften'd the stones;—"

Lay by these:—

[Sings.]

>   "Sing willow, willow, willow;—"

Pr'ythee, hie thee; he'll come anon:—

[Sings.]

>   "Sing all a green willow must be my garland.
>   Let nobody blame him; his scorn I approve,—"

Nay, that's not next.—Hark! who is't that knocks?

EMILIA.

It's the wind.

DESDEMONA.

[Sings.]

>   "I call'd my love false love; but what said he then?
>   Sing willow, willow, willow:
>   'If I court mo women, you'll couch with mo men.'"

So get thee gone; good night. Mine eyes do itch;
Doth that bode weeping?

EMILIA.

'Tis neither here nor there.

DESDEMONA.

I have heard it said so.—O, these men, these men!—
Dost thou in conscience think,—tell me, Emilia,—
That there be women do abuse their husbands
In such gross kind?

EMILIA.

There be some such, no question.

DESDEMONA.

Wouldst thou do such a deed for all the world?

EMILIA.

Why, would not you?

DESDEMONA.

No, by this heavenly light!

EMILIA.

Nor I neither by this heavenly light; I might do't as well i' the dark.

DESDEMONA.

Wouldst thou do such a deed for all the world?

EMILIA.

The world's a huge thing; it is a great price
For a small vice.

DESDEMONA.

In troth, I think thou wouldst not.

EMILIA.

In troth, I think I should; and undo't when I had done. Marry, I would not do such a thing for a joint-ring, nor for measures of lawn, nor for gowns, petticoats, nor caps, nor any petty exhibition; but, for the whole world—why, who would not make her husband a cuckold to make him a monarch? I should venture purgatory for't.

DESDEMONA.

Beshrew me, if I would do such a wrong for the whole world.

EMILIA.

Why, the wrong is but a wrong i' the world; and having the world for your labor, 'tis a wrong in your own world, and you might quickly make it right.

DESDEMONA.

I do not think there is any such woman.

EMILIA.

Yes, a dozen; and as many to the vantage as would store
the world they play'd for.
But I do think it is their husbands' faults
If wives do fall: say that they slack their duties
And pour our treasures into foreign laps;
Or else break out in peevish jealousies,
Throwing restraint upon us; or say they strike us,
Or scant our former having in despite;
Why, we have galls; and though we have some grace,
Yet have we some revenge. Let husbands know
Their wives have sense like them: they see and smell

And have their palates both for sweet and sour,
As husbands have. What is it that they do
When they change us for others? Is it sport?
I think it is: and doth affection breed it?
I think it doth: is't frailty that thus errs?
It is so too. And have not we affections,
Desires for sport, and frailty, as men have?
Then let them use us well: else let them know
The ills we do their ills instruct us so.

DESDEMONA.

Good-night, good-night: heaven me such usage send,
Not to pick bad from bad, but by bad mend!

[Exeunt.

ACT V.

SCENE I. *Cyprus. A Street.*

Enter IAGO *and* RODERIGO.

IAGO.

Here, stand behind this bulk; straight will he come:
Wear thy good rapier bare, and put it home:
Quick, quick; fear nothing; I'll be at thy elbow:
It makes us, or it mars us; think on that,
And fix most firm thy resolution.

RODERIGO.

Be near at hand; I may miscarry in't.

IAGO.

Here, at thy hand: be bold, and take thy stand.
[Retires to a little distance.]

RODERIGO.

I have no great devotion to the deed;
And yet he hath given me satisfying reasons:—
'Tis but a man gone.—Forth, my sword; he dies.
[Goes to his stand.]

IAGO.

I have rubb'd this young quat almost to the sense,
And he grows angry. Now, whether he kill Cassio,
Or Cassio him, or each do kill the other,
Every way makes my gain: live Roderigo,
He calls me to a restitution large
Of gold and jewels that I bobb'd from him,
As gifts to Desdemona;
It must not be: if Cassio do remain,
He hath a daily beauty in his life
That makes me ugly; and besides, the Moor
May unfold me to him; there stand I in much peril;
No, he must die.—But, so, I hear him coming.
Enter CASSIO.

Cassio.   I will make proof of thine.
Roderigo.   Oh, I am slain!
                                 Act V.   Scene I.

RODERIGO.
I know his gait; 'tis he.—Villain, thou diest!

[Rushes out, and makes a pass at CASSIO.*]*

CASSIO.

That thrust had been mine enemy indeed,
But that my coat is better than thou know'st:
I will make proof of thine.

[Draws, and wounds RODERIGO.*]*

RODERIGO.

O, I am slain!

[Iago rushes from his post, cuts Cassio behind in the leg, and exit.]

CASSIO.

I am maim'd forever.—Help, ho! murder! murder!

[Falls.]

Enter OTHELLO *at a distance.*

OTHELLO.

The voice of Cassio: Iago keeps his word.

RODERIGO.

O, villain that I am!

OTHELLO.

It is even so.

CASSIO.

O, help, ho! light! a surgeon!

OTHELLO.

'Tis he:—O brave Iago, honest and just,
That hast such noble sense of thy friend's wrong!
Thou teachest me,—minion, your dear lies dead,
And your unbless'd fate hies. Strumpet, I come!
Forth of my heart those charms, thine eyes, are blotted;
Thy bed, lust-stain'd, shall with lust's blood be spotted.

[Exit.

Enter LODOVICO *and* GRATIANO *at a distance.*

CASSIO.

What, ho! no watch? no passage? murder! murder!

GRATIANO.

'Tis some mischance; the cry is very direful.

CASSIO.

O, help!

LODOVICO.

Hark!

RODERIGO.

O wretched villain!

LODOVICO.

Two or three groan:—it is a heavy night:
These may be counterfeits: let's think't unsafe
To come in to the cry without more help.

RODERIGO.

Nobody come? then shall I bleed to death.

LODOVICO.

Hark!

Re-enter IAGO, *with a light.*

GRATIANO.

Here's one comes in his shirt, with light and weapons.

IAGO.

Who's there? whose noise is this that cries on murder?

LODOVICO.

We do not know.

IAGO.

Did not you hear a cry?

CASSIO.

Here, here! for heaven's sake, help me!

IAGO.

What's the matter?

GRATIANO.

This is Othello's ancient, as I take it.

LODOVICO.

The same indeed; a very valiant fellow.

IAGO.

What are you here that cry so grievously?

CASSIO.

Iago? O, I am spoil'd, undone by villains!
Give me some help.

IAGO.

O me, lieutenant! what villains have done this?

CASSIO.

I think that one of them is hereabout,
And cannot make away.

IAGO.

O treacherous villains!—

[To LODOVICO *and* GRATIANO.*]* What are you there?

Come in and give some help.

RODERIGO.

O, help me here!

CASSIO.

That's one of them.

IAGO.

O murderous slave! O villain!
[Stabs RODERIGO.*]*

RODERIGO.

O damn'd Iago! O inhuman dog!

IAGO.

Kill men i' the dark!—Where be these bloody thieves?—
How silent is this town!—Ho! murder! murder!—
What may you be? are you of good or evil?

LODOVICO.

As you shall prove us, praise us.

IAGO.

Signior Lodovico?

LODOVICO.

He, sir.

IAGO.

I cry you mercy. Here's Cassio hurt by villains.

GRATIANO.

Cassio!

IAGO.

How is't, brother?

CASSIO.

My leg is cut in two.

IAGO.

Marry, heaven forbid!—
Light, gentlemen:—I'll bind it with my shirt.

Enter BIANCA.

BIANCA.

What is the matter, ho? who is't that cried?

IAGO.

Who is't that cried!

BIANCA.

O my dear Cassio, my sweet Cassio! O Cassio, Cassio, Cassio!

IAGO.

O notable strumpet!—Cassio, may you suspect
Who they should be that have thus mangled you?

CASSIO.

No.

GRATIANO.

I am sorry to find you thus: I have been to seek you.

IAGO.

Lend me a garter:—so.—O, for a chair,
To bear him easily hence!

BIANCA.

Alas, he faints!—O Cassio, Cassio, Cassio!

IAGO.

Gentlemen all, I do suspect this trash
To be a party in this injury.—
Patience awhile, good Cassio.—Come, come;
Lend me a light.—Know we this face or no?
Alas, my friend and my dear countryman
Roderigo? no:—yes, sure; O heaven! Roderigo.

GRATIANO.

What, of Venice?

IAGO.

Even he, sir: did you know him?

GRATIANO.

Know him! ay.

IAGO.

Signior Gratiano? I cry you gentle pardon;
These bloody accidents must excuse my manners,
That so neglected you.

GRATIANO.

I am glad to see you.

IAGO.

How do you, Cassio?—O, a chair, a chair!

GRATIANO.

Roderigo!

IAGO.

He, he, 'tis he.—*[A chair brought in.]* O, that's well said;
—the chair:—
Some good man bear him carefully from hence;
I'll fetch the general's surgeon. *[To* BIANCA.*]* For you, mistress,
Save you your labour.—He that lies slain here, Cassio,
Was my dear friend: what malice was between you?

CASSIO.

None in the world; nor do I know the man.

IAGO.

[To BIANCA.*]* What, look you pale?—O, bear him out o' the air.
*[*CASSIO *and* RODERIGO *are borne off.]*
Stay you, good gentlemen.—Look you pale, mistress?—
Do you perceive the gastness of her eye?—
Nay, if you stare, we shall hear more anon.—
Behold her well; I pray you, look upon her:
Do you see, gentlemen? nay, guiltiness will speak
Though tongues were out of use.

Enter EMILIA.

EMILIA.

'Las, what's the matter? what's the matter, husband?

IAGO.

Cassio hath here been set on in the dark
By Roderigo, and fellows that are 'scap'd:
He's almost slain, and Roderigo dead.

EMILIA.

Alas, good gentleman! alas, good Cassio!

IAGO.

This is the fruit of whoring.—Pr'ythee, Emilia,
Go know of Cassio where he supp'd to-night.—
What, do you shake at that?

BIANCA.

He supp'd at my house; but I therefore shake not.

IAGO.

O, did he so? I charge you, go with me.

EMILIA.

Fie, fie upon thee, strumpet!

BIANCA.

I am no strumpet, but of life as honest
As you that thus abuse me.

EMILIA.

As I! foh! fie upon thee!

IAGO.

Kind gentlemen, let's go see poor Cassio dress'd.—
Come, mistress, you must tell's another tale.—
Emilia, run you to the citadel,
And tell my lord and lady what hath happ'd.—
Will you go on, I pray? *[Aside.]* This is the night
That either makes me or fordoes me quite.

[Exeunt.

SCENE II. *Cyprus. A Bedchamber in the castle: Desdemona
in bed asleep; a light burning.*

Enter OTHELLO.

OTHELLO.

It is the cause, it is the cause, my soul,—
Let me not name it to you, you chaste stars!—
It is the cause.—Yet I'll not shed her blood;
Nor scar that whiter skin of hers than snow,
And smooth as monumental alabaster.
[Takes off his sword.]
Yet she must die, else she'll betray more men.
Put out the light, and then put out the light:
If I quench thee, thou flaming minister,

I can again thy former light restore,
Should I repent me:—but once put out thy light,
Thou cunning'st pattern of excelling nature,
I know not where is that Promethean heat
That can thy light relume. When I have pluck'd thy rose,
I cannot give it vital growth again,
It must needs wither:—I'll smell it on the tree.—
[Kissing her.]

O, balmy breath, that dost almost persuade
Justice to break her sword!—One more, one more;—
Be thus when thou art dead, and I will kill thee,
And love thee after.—One more, and this the last;
So sweet was ne'er so fatal. I must weep,
But they are cruel tears: this sorrow's heavenly;
It strikes where it doth love.—She wakes.

DESDEMONA.

Who's there? Othello?

OTHELLO.

Ay, Desdemona.

DESDEMONA.

Will you come to bed, my lord?

OTHELLO.

Have you pray'd to-night, Desdemona?

DESDEMONA.

Ay, my lord.

OTHELLO.

If you bethink yourself of any crime
Unreconcil'd as yet to heaven and grace,
Solicit for it straight.

DESDEMONA.

Alack, my lord, what may you mean by that?

OTHELLO.

Well, do it, and be brief; I will walk by.
I would not kill thy unprepared spirit;
No,—heaven forfend!—I would not kill thy soul.

DESDEMONA.

Talk you of killing?

Othello.   Have you pray'd to-night, Desdemona?
Desdemona.   Ay, my lord.   *Act V.   Scene II*

OTHELLO.
Ay, I do.

DESDEMONA.
Then heaven have mercy on me!

OTHELLO.
Amen, with all my heart!

DESDEMONA.
If you say so, I hope you will not kill me.

OTHELLO.
Hum!

DESDEMONA.
And yet I fear you; for you are fatal then
When your eyes roll so: why I should fear I know not,
Since guiltiness I know not; but yet I feel I fear.

OTHELLO.
Think on thy sins.

DESDEMONA.

They are loves I bear to you.

OTHELLO.

Ay, and for that thou diest.

DESDEMONA.

That death's unnatural that kills for loving.—
Alas, why gnaw you so your nether lip?
Some bloody passion shakes your very frame:
These are portents; but yet I hope, I hope,
They do not point on me.

OTHELLO.

Peace, and be still!

DESDEMONA.

I will so. What's the matter?

OTHELLO.

That handkerchief which I so loved and gave thee
Thou gav'st to Cassio.

DESDEMONA.

No, by my life and soul!
Send for the man, and ask him.

OTHELLO.

Sweet soul, take heed,
Take heed of perjury; thou'rt on thy death-bed.

DESDEMONA.

Ay, but not yet to die.

OTHELLO.

Yes, presently:
Therefore confess thee freely of thy sin;
For to deny each article with oath
Cannot remove nor choke the strong conception
That I do groan withal. Thou art to die.

DESDEMONA.

Then, Lord have mercy on me!

OTHELLO.

I say, amen.

DESDEMONA.

And have you mercy too!—I never did
Offend you in my life; never lov'd Cassio

But with such general warranty of heaven
As I might love: I never gave him token.

> OTHELLO.

By heaven, I saw my handkerchief in 's hand.
O perjur'd woman! thou dost stone my heart,
And mak'st me call what I intend to do
A murder, which I thought a sacrifice:
I saw the handkerchief.

> DESDEMONA.

He found it then;
I never gave it him:—send for him hither;
Let him confess a truth.

> OTHELLO.

He hath confess'd.

> DESDEMONA.

What, my lord?

> OTHELLO.

That he hath us'd thee.

> DESDEMONA.

How? unlawfully?

> OTHELLO.

Ay.

> DESDEMONA.

He will not say so.

> OTHELLO.

No, his mouth is stopp'd;
Honest Iago hath ta'en order for't.

> DESDEMONA.

O, my fear interprets!—What, is he dead?

> OTHELLO.

Had all his hairs been lives, my great revenge
Had stomach for them all.

> DESDEMONA.

Alas, he is betray'd, and I undone!

> OTHELLO.

Out, strumpet! Weep'st thou for him to my face?

DESDEMONA.

O, banish me, my lord, but kill me not!

OTHELLO.

Down, strumpet!

DESDEMONA.

Kill me to-morrow; let me live to-night!

OTHELLO.

Nay, if you strive,—

DESDEMONA.

But half an hour!

OTHELLO.

Being done, there is no pause.

DESDEMONA.

But while I say one prayer!

OTHELLO.

It is too late.

[Smothers her.]

EMILIA.

[Within.] My lord, my lord! what, ho! my lord, my lord!

OTHELLO.

What noise is this?—Not dead? not yet quite dead?
I that am cruel am yet merciful;
I would not have thee linger in thy pain:—
So, so.

EMILIA.

[Within.] What, ho! my lord, my lord!

OTHELLO.

Who's there?

EMILIA.

[Within.] O, good my lord, I would speak a word with you!

OTHELLO.

Yes:—'tis Emilia:—by and by.—She's dead.—
'Tis like she comes to speak of Cassio's death;
The noise was high.—Ha! no more moving?
Still as the grave.—Shall she come in?—Were't good?—
I think she stirs again:—no.—What's best to do?

If she come in, she'll sure speak to my wife:
My wife! my wife! what wife? I have no wife.
O, insupportable! O heavy hour!
Methinks it should be now a huge eclipse
Of sun and moon, and that the affrighted globe
Should yawn at alteration.

EMILIA.

[Within.] I do beseech you
That I may speak with you, O, good my lord!

OTHELLO.

I had forgot thee: O, come in, Emilia:—
Soft,—by and by:—let me the curtains draw.—
Where art thou?

[Unlocks the door.]

Enter EMILIA.

What's the matter with thee now?

EMILIA.

O, my good lord, yonder's foul murders done!

OTHELLO.

What, now?

EMILIA.

But now, my lord.

OTHELLO.

It is the very error of the moon;
She comes more nearer earth than she was wont
And makes men mad.

EMILIA.

Cassio, my lord, hath kill'd a young Venetian
Call'd Roderigo.

OTHELLO.

Roderigo kill'd?
And Cassio kill'd?

EMILIA.

No, Cassio is not kill'd.

OTHELLO.

Not Cassio kill'd! then murder's out of tune,
And sweet revenge grows harsh.

DESDEMONA.

O, falsely, falsely murder'd!

EMILIA.

Alas, what cry is that?

OTHELLO.

That! what?

EMILIA.

Out, and alas! That was my lady's voice.—
Help! help, ho! help!—O lady, speak again!
Sweet Desdemona! O sweet mistress, speak!

DESDEMONA.

A guiltless death I die.

EMILIA.

O, who hath done this deed?

DESDEMONA.

Nobody; I myself. Farewell:
Commend me to my kind lord: O, farewell!

[Dies.

OTHELLO.

Why, how should she be murder'd?

EMILIA.

Alas, who knows?

OTHELLO.

You heard her say herself it was not I.

EMILIA.

She said so: I must needs report the truth.

OTHELLO.

She's like a liar, gone to burning hell:
'Twas I that kill'd her.

EMILIA.

O, the more angel she,
And you the blacker devil!

OTHELLO.

She turn'd to folly, and she was a whore.

EMILIA.

Thou dost belie her, and thou art a devil.

OTHELLO.

She was false as water.

EMILIA.

Thou art rash as fire, to say
That she was false: O, she was heavenly true!

OTHELLO.

Cassio did win her; ask thy husband else.
O, I were damn'd beneath all depth in hell,
But that I did proceed upon just grounds
To this extremity. Thy husband knew it all.

EMILIA.

My husband!

OTHELLO.

Thy husband.

EMILIA.

That she was false to wedlock?

OTHELLO.

Ay, with Cassio. Nay, had she been true,
If heaven would make me such another world
Of one entire and perfect chrysolite,
I'd not have sold her for it.

EMILIA.

My husband!

OTHELLO.

Ay, 'twas he that told me first:
An honest man he is, and hates the slime
That sticks on filthy deeds.

EMILIA.

My husband!

OTHELLO.

What needs this iterance, woman? I say thy husband.

EMILIA.

O mistress, villainy hath made mocks with love!—
My husband say that she was false!

OTHELLO.

He, woman;
I say thy husband: dost understand the word?
My friend, thy husband, honest, honest Iago.

Emilia. I care not for thy sword; I 'll make thee known,
Though I lost twenty lives.—Help! help, ho! help!
The Moor has kill'd my mistress! Murder! murder!

Act V. Scene II

EMILIA.

If he say so, may his pernicious soul
Rot half a grain a day! he lies to the heart:
She was too fond of her most filthy bargain.

OTHELLO.

Ha!

EMILIA.

Do thy worst:
This deed of thine is no more worthy heaven
Than thou wast worthy her.

OTHELLO.

Peace, you were best.

EMILIA.

Thou hast not half that power to do me harm
As I have to be hurt. O gull! O dolt!
As ignorant as dirt! thou hast done a deed,—
I care not for thy sword; I'll make thee known,
Though I lost twenty lives.—Help! help, ho! help!
The Moor hath kill'd my mistress! murder, murder!

Enter MONTANO, GRATIANO, *and* IAGO.

MONTANO.

What is the matter?—How now, general!

EMILIA.

O, are you come, Iago? you have done well,
That men must lay their murders on your neck.

GRATIANO.

What is the matter?

EMILIA.

Disprove this villain, if thou be'st a man:
He says thou told'st him that his wife was false:
I know thou didst not, thou'rt not such a villain:
Speak, for my heart is full.

IAGO.

I told him what I thought; and told no more
Than what he found himself was apt and true.

EMILIA.

But did you ever tell him she was false?

IAGO.

I did.

EMILIA.

You told a lie; an odious, damned lie;
Upon my soul, a lie; a wicked lie:—
She false with Cassio!—Did you say with Cassio?

IAGO.

With Cassio, mistress. Go to, charm your tongue.

EMILIA.

I will not charm my tongue; I am bound to speak:
My mistress here lies murder'd in her bed,—

ALL.

O heavens forfend!

EMILIA.

And your reports have set the murder on.

OTHELLO.

Nay, stare not, masters: it is true, indeed.

GRATIANO.

'Tis a strange truth.

MONTANO.

O monstrous act!

EMILIA.

Villany, villany, villany!
I think upon't,—I think,—I smell't;—O villany!—
I thought so then;—I'll kill myself for grief:—
O villany, villany!

IAGO.

What, are you mad? I charge you, get you home.

EMILIA.

Good gentlemen, let me have leave to speak:
'Tis proper I obey him, but not now.—
Perchance, Iago, I will ne'er go home.

OTHELLO.

O! O! O!

[Hanging over his wife.]

EMILIA.

Nay, lay thee down and roar;
For thou hast kill'd the sweetest innocent
That e'er did lift up eye.

OTHELLO.

[Rising.] O, she was foul!—
I scarce did know you, uncle; there lies your niece,

Whose breath, indeed, these hands have newly stopp'd:
I know this act shows horrible and grim.

GRATIANO.

Poor Desdemona! I am glad thy father's dead:
Thy match was mortal to him, and pure grief
Shore his old thread in twain: did he live now,
This sight would make him do a desperate turn,
Yea, curse his better angel from his side,
And fall to reprobance.

OTHELLO.

'Tis pitiful; but yet Iago knows
That she with Cassio hath the act of shame
A thousand times committed; Cassio confess'd it:
And she did gratify his amorous works
With that recognizance and pledge of love
Which I first gave her; I saw it in his hand:
It was a handkerchief, an antique token
My father gave my mother.

EMILIA.

O heaven! O heavenly powers!

IAGO.

Come, hold your peace.

EMILIA.

'Twill out, 'twill out:—I peace!
No, I will speak as liberal as the north:
Let heaven and men and devils, let them all,
All, all, cry shame against me, yet I'll speak.

IAGO.

Be wise, and get you home.

EMILIA.

I will not.
[IAGO *offers to stab his wife.*]

GRATIANO.

Fie!
Your sword upon a woman?

EMILIA.

O thou dull Moor! that handkerchief thou speak'st of
I found by fortune and did give my husband;

For often with a solemn earnestness,—
More than, indeed, belong'd to such a trifle,—
He begg'd of me to steal it.

IAGO.

Villanous whore!

EMILIA.

She give it Cassio! no, alas, I found it,
And I did give't my husband.

IAGO.

Filth, thou liest!

EMILIA.

By heaven, I do not, I do not, gentlemen.—
O murderous coxcomb! What should such a fool
Do with so good a wife?

OTHELLO.

Are there not stones in heaven
But what serve for thunder?—Precious villain!

[IAGO *stabs* EMILIA, *and then runs out.*

GRATIANO.

The woman falls; sure, he hath kill'd his wife.

EMILIA.

Ay, ay:—O, lay me by my mistress' side.

GRATIANO.

He's gone, but his wife's kill'd.

MONTANO.

'Tis a notorious villain. Take you this weapon,
Which I have here recover'd from the Moor:
Come, guard the door without; let him not pass,
But kill him rather. I'll after that same villain,
For 'tis a damned slave.

[*Exit* MONTANO *and* GRATIANO.

OTHELLO.

I am not valiant neither,
But every puny whipster gets my sword:—
But why should honor outlive honesty?
Let it go all.

EMILIA.

What did thy song bode, lady?
Hark, canst thou hear me? I will play the swan,
And die in music:—
[Sings.] "Willow, willow, willow."
Moor, she was chaste; she lov'd thee, cruel Moor;
So come my soul to bliss, as I speak true;
So speaking as I think, I die,—I die.

[Dies.

OTHELLO.

I have another weapon in this chamber;
It is a sword of Spain, the ice-brook's temper:—
O, here it is.—Uncle, I must come forth.

GRATIANO.

[Within.] If thou attempt it, it will cost thee dear:
Thou hast no weapon, and perforce must suffer.

OTHELLO.

Look in upon me then, and speak with me,
Or, naked as I am, I will assault thee.

Re-enter GRATIANO.

GRATIANO.

What is the matter?

OTHELLO.

Behold, I have a weapon;
A better never did itself sustain
Upon a soldier's thigh: I have seen the day
That with this little arm and this good sword
I have made my way through more impediments
Than twenty times your stop:—but, O vain boast!
Who can control his fate? 'tis not so now.—
Be not afraid, though you do see me weapon'd;
Here is my journey's end, here is my butt,
And very sea-mark of my utmost sail.
Do you go back dismay'd? 'tis a lost fear;
Man but a rush against Othello's breast,
And he retires:—where should Othello go?—
Now, how dost thou look now? O ill-starr'd wench!
Pale as thy smock! When we shall meet at compt,
This look of thine will hurl my soul from heaven,

And fiends will snatch at it. Cold, cold, my girl!
Even like thy chastity.—
O cursed, cursed slave!—Whip me, ye devils,
From the possession of this heavenly sight!
Blow me about in winds! roast me in sulphur!
Wash me in steep-down gulfs of liquid fire!—
O Desdemona! dead, Desdemona! dead! Oh, oh, oh!

[Enter Lodovico, Montano, Cassio *carried in a chair, and Officers*
with Iago *prisoner.]*

Lodovico.
Where is this rash and most unfortunate man?

Othello.
That's he that was Othello;—here I am.

Lodovico.
Where is that viper? bring the villain forth.

Othello.
I look down towards his feet;—but that's a fable.—
If that thou be'st a devil, I cannot kill thee.
[Wounds Iago.*]*

Lodovico.
Wrench his sword from him.

Iago.
I bleed, sir, but not kill'd.

Othello.
I am not sorry neither: I'd have thee live;
For, in my sense, 'tis happiness to die.

Lodovico.
O thou Othello, that wert once so good,
Fall'n in the practice of a damned slave,
What shall be said to thee?

Othello.
Why, anything;
An honorable murderer, if you will;
For naught did I in hate, but all in honor.

Lodovico.
This wretch hath part confess'd his villany:
Did you and he consent in Cassio's death?

OTHELLO.

Ay.

CASSIO.

Dear general, I never gave you cause.

OTHELLO.

I do believe it, and I ask your pardon.
Will you, I pray, demand that demi-devil
Why he hath thus ensnar'd my soul and body?

IAGO.

Demand me nothing: what you know, you know:
From this time forth I never will speak word.

LODOVICO.

What, not to pray?

GRATIANO.

Torments will ope your lips.

OTHELLO.

Well, thou dost best.

LODOVICO.

Sir, you shall understand what hath befall'n,
Which, as I think, you know not. Here is a letter
Found in the pocket of the slain Roderigo,
And here another: the one of them imports
The death of Cassio to be undertook
By Roderigo.

OTHELLO.

O villain!

CASSIO.

Most heathenish and most gross!

LODOVICO.

Now here's another discontented paper,
Found in his pocket too; and this, it seems,
Roderigo meant to have sent this damned villain;
But that, belike, Iago in the interim
Came in and satisfied him.

OTHELLO.

O the pernicious caitiff!—
How came you, Cassio, by that handkerchief
That was my wife's?

Cassio.

I found it in my chamber;
And he himself confess'd but even now
That there he dropp'd it for a special purpose
Which wrought to his desire.

Othello.

O fool! fool! fool!

Cassio.

There is besides in Roderigo's letter,—
How he upbraids Iago, that he made him
Brave me upon the watch; whereon it came
That I was cast: and even but now he spake,
After long seeming dead,—Iago hurt him,
Iago set him on.

Lodovico.

You must forsake this room, and go with us:
Your power and your command is taken off,
And Cassio rules in Cyprus. For this slave,—
If there be any cunning cruelty
That can torment him much and hold him long,
It shall be his. You shall close prisoner rest,
Till that the nature of your fault be known
To the Venetian state.—Come, bring away.

Othello.

Soft you; a word or two before you go.
I have done the state some service, and they know't.—
No more of that.—I pray you, in your letters,
When you shall these unlucky deeds relate,
Speak of me as I am; nothing extenuate,
Nor set down aught in malice: then must you speak
Of one that loved not wisely, but too well;
Of one not easily jealous, but, being wrought,
Perplex'd in the extreme; of one whose hand,
Like the base Indian, threw a pearl away
Richer than all his tribe; of one whose subdu'd eyes,
Albeit unused to the melting mood,
Drop tears as fast as the Arabian trees
Their medicinal gum. Set you down this;
And say besides,—that in Aleppo once,
Where a malignant and a turban'd Turk

Beat a Venetian and traduc'd the state,
I took by the throat the circumcised dog
And smote him—thus.
[Stabs himself.]

LODOVICO.

O bloody period!

GRATIANO.

All that's spoke is marr'd.

OTHELLO.

I kiss'd thee ere I kill'd thee:—no way but this,
Killing myself, to die upon a kiss. *[Falling upon* DESDEMONA.*]*

CASSIO.

This did I fear, but thought he had no weapon;
For he was great of heart.

LODOVICO.

[To IAGO.*]* O Spartan dog,
More fell than anguish, hunger, or the sea!
Look on the tragic loading of this bed;
This is thy work:—the object poisons sight;
Let it be hid.—Gratiano, keep the house,
And seize upon the fortunes of the Moor,
For they succeed on you.—To you, lord governor,
Remains the censure of this hellish villain;
The time, the place, the torture,—O, enforce it!
Myself will straight aboard; and to the state
This heavy act with heavy heart relate.

[Exeunt.

THE END

Made in the USA
Monee, IL
05 July 2021